Economic Mavericks:
The Texas Institutionalists

POLITICAL ECONOMY
AND PUBLIC POLICY, VOLUME 9

Editors: William Breit, *Department of Economics, Trinity University,*
San Antonio, and
Kenneth G. Elzinga, *Department of Economics, University*
of Virginia

Political Economy and Public Policy

An International Series of Monographs
in Law and Economics, History of Economic Thought
and Public Finance

Edited by **William Breit**,
Department of Economics,
Trinity University
and **Kenneth G. Elzinga,**
*Department of Economics,
University of Virginia*

Volume 1. **Contemporary Economists In Perspective**

Edited by **Henry W. Spiegel**, *Catholic University of America*
and **Warren J. Samuels,** *Michigan State University*

Volume 2. **Methodological Controversy in Economics:
Historical Essays in Honor of T.W. Hutchison**

Edited by **A.W. Coats**, *The University of Nottingham*

Volume 3. **Law, Economics and Public Policy**

Nicholas Mercuro and **Timothy Ryan**, *Department of
Economics and Finance, University of New Orleans*

Volume 4. **Monitoring and Compliance:
The Political Economy of Inspection**

David Hemenway, *Department of Health Policy
and Management, Havard University*

Volume 5. **Public Expenditure Decisions:
Behavior, Institutions, Procedures and Performance**

Earl R. Brubaker, *Naval Postgraduate School*

Volume 6. **Public Choice and Constitutional Economics**

Edited by **James D. Gwartney** and **Richard E. Wagner**,
Florida State University

Volume 7. **The Political Legitimacy of Markets
and Governments**

Edited by **Thomas R. Dye,** *The Florida State University*

Volume 8. **The Problem of the Multiple Interpretations of Ricardo**

Ercument G. Aksoy, *Department of Economics,
California State University, Fullerton*

Economic Mavericks:
The Texas Institutionalists

by **RONNIE J. PHILLIPS**
Colorado State University

 **JAI PRESS INC.**

Greenwich, Connecticut   *London, England*

HB
119
A3
P48
1995

Library of Congress Cataloging-in-Publication Data

Phillips, Ronnie J. 1951-
   Economic mavericks : the Texas Institutionalists / by Ronnie J.
Phillips.
      p.   cm.—(Political economy and public policy; v. 9)
      Includes bibliographical references and index.
      ISBN 1-55938-467-0
      1. Economicsts—Texas—Biography.   2. University of Texas. Dept.
of Economics—History.   3. Institutional economics—History.
I.   Title.   II. Series.
HB119.A3P48.   1995
330'.092'2764—dc20

                                                     95-40572

CONTENTS

List of Contributors   ix

I.   Introduction
      Ronnie J. Phillips   1

II.   The Ayresian Legacy
      *James Ronald Stanfield and
      Jacqueline Bloom Stanfield*   7

III. E. E. Hale on Economic Theory and the Real World
      Ronnie J. Phillips   31

IV.   Robert Montgomery: A Gentle Iconoclast in
         Industrial Organization
      Robert Kling   51

V.   Ruth Allen: Frontier Labor Economist
      Alexandra Bernasek and Douglas Kinnear   75

VI.   Alton Wiley: The Most Complete Economist
      Gerald F. Vaughn   107

VII. Erich W. Zimmerman: The Dynamics of Resourceship
      Stephen L. McDonald   151

Bibliography   185

Index   197

LIST OF CONTRIBUTORS

Alexandra Bernasek

Department of Economics
Colorado State University

Douglas Kinnear

Department of Economics
Colorado State University

Robert Kling

Department of Economics
Colorado State University

Stephen L. McDonald

Department of Economics
The University of Texas
at Austin

Ronnie J. Phillips

Department of Economics
Colorado State University

James Ronald Stanfield

Department of Economics
Colorado State University

Jaqueline Bloom Stanfield

Department of Sociology
University of Northern
Colorado

Gerald A. Vaughn

Resource Economics and
Policy
University of Delaware

Department of Economics
The University of Texas at Austin
1955

Left to Right

Seated: Robert H. Montgomery, Clarence Alton Wiley, Clarence Edwin Ayres, Wendel C. Gordon, Ruth A. Allen, Edward Everett Hale, Eastin Nelson

Standing: C. P. Blair, Stephen L. McDonald, Carey C. Thompson, Donald McClung, Matthew Jonas, Frederic Meyers

Individual photo:
Erich Zimmermann

Chapter 1

Introduction

Ronnie J. Phillips

I have been allowing myself to dream of the possibility of the development in the course of the next few years of a sort of 'Texas school'.

—Clarence Edwin Ayres, 1934

In 1870s Texas, most cattlemen branded their cattle as a means of determining ownership. One cattleman, by the name of Samuel Maverick, refused to brand his cattle, however. When his herd was stampeded with neighboring cattle, and they were all subsequently rounded up, unbranded cattle were claimed as *Maverick's*. Today the dictionary defines maverick as "an independent individual who refuses to conform with his group." This volume of essays examines the contributions of individuals who were *economic mavericks*. Each taught at The University of Texas at Austin (UT) in the period roughly spanning from the Great Depression of the 1930s to the New Frontier of the 1960s. Clarence Edwin Ayres, Edward Everett Hale, Robert W. Montgomery, Ruth Alice Allen, Clarence Alton Wiley, and Erich W. Zimmermann comprised what has become known as the 'Texas School of Institutional Economics'. These individuals were the major force in the economics department

1

at UT and each made lasting contributions through their
teachings and writings to the development of economic theory
and policy.

The members of the Texas school were first of all economists.
Their contributions were not outside the mainstream of
economics, rather their contributions were independent of what
the mainstream of the economics profession was doing at the
time. In numerous instances they anticipated theoretical and
policy debates in economics by more than two decades. For
example, Clarence Ayres wrote of the importance of human
capital in economic development, Robert Montgomery
advocated marginal cost pricing for utilities, Ruth Allen spoke
of the importance of gender roles in the economy, and Erich
Zimmermann articulated the functional approach to resources.
Samuel Maverick was a cattleman, but he refused to go along
with what other cattlemen were doing. The same is true of the
economists discussed in the present volume: they were
economists, but they refused to be shackled by the established
methodology and policy analysis of the economics profession.

They were not ivory tower theorists. This did not mean that
they forsook all theory, rather theory and policy in the real
world were intimately tied together. When Ayres made the
statement about the possibility of a 'Texas school', he was
trying to persuade George W. Stocking, who had left Texas
for the Antitrust Division in the Justice Department, to return
to UT. The New Deal was destined to have an important
impact on institutionalism in academics, and many of the
members of the economics department at UT put in short
stints during the 1930s. Texas was not unusual, for at other
universities, such as Columbia, institutionalist economists
moved from academia to the "real world" of government
service during the New Deal. This included the senior
acknowledged leaders of the institutionalist school such as
Walton Hamilton. Many who had studied with Thorstein
Veblen, John R. Commons, and Wesley Mitchell became
active in the New Deal: Adolf Berle, Henry Wallace, Gardiner
Means, Isadore Lubin, Thurman Arnold, and Mordecai
Ezekial, among others. The formulators of New Deal

industrial and agricultural policy—Roosevelt's Brain Trust—were institutionalists, and the early New Deal can be viewed as putting institutionalism into practice (Rosen 1977, p. 206).

William Breit, among others, has noted that institutionalism peaked in the 1930s, and seemed to decline after that (Breit 1988). The exodus of the institutionalists from academia to the "real world" of policy may have had an impact on the subsequent evolution of economics. There may be a strong connection between the drawing of institutionalists into the New Deal and the decline of institutionalism in graduate programs in economics at American universities. After the 1930s, institutionalism waned at universities where previously it had figured prominently: Chicago, Harvard, and Columbia.

The contributors to the present volume were asked not to write essays which merely praised the contributions of these individuals but to explicitly assess whether their contributions have withstood the test of time. In other words, are the issues they addressed and the policies they recommended of continuing interest? In many instances, it will be seen that though they were ahead of their time in making certain policy recommendations, not surprisingly changing circumstances force a reassessment of their policy conclusions.

The purpose of examining the contributions of the Texas School is not to argue that they found eternal truths; rather, it is to point out to those who have not previously known of their contributions how the Texas economists were able to make these contributions by using an approach which differed from that of their generation of economists. The rise of the "new institutional economics" and the important contributions of individuals such as Nobel Prize winner Douglass C. North, have once again brought economics back to the study of institutions and to territory explored earlier by the Texas institutionalists.

The members of the Texas school studied the interaction between technological change and the institutional structure of society. They were concerned with the failures of laissez faire and how government policy might improve the welfare of society. If there is one fundamental lesson to be learned from the work of the Texas school, it is that economic theory cannot develop in a vacuum apart from the real working lives of the average person. Economists must directly address issues which affect the lives and livelihoods of people.

The essay by James Ronald Stanfield and Jacqueline Bloom Stanfield sets forth the underlying methodology of the Texas School as articulated by Clarence Ayres. Though Ayres was trained as a philosopher, he taught in an economics department. This was not unusual at the time and it is important to point out that his lifelong friend and Chicago classmate, Frank Knight, was also a philosopher. Ayres developed and adapted John Dewey's instrumental theory of knowledge and elaborated upon Thorstein Veblen's dichotomy between the dynamic force of technology and the static force of ceremony. Edward Everett Hale taught history of economic thought. He was an early advocate of Keynesian economic theory and policy. Hale's message was the importance of the connection between the development of economic theory and the real world. The chapter on Hale evaluates his thesis in the history of economic thought and in contemporary times.

Robert Montgomery made important contributions to Industrial Organization theory. Robert Kling in his chapter sets forth policy prescriptions advocated by Montgomery and evaluates their relevance today. Some of Montgomery's contributions became conventional wisdom, while others have yet to be fully appreciated.

Ruth Allen was one of the few women economists at the full professor rank during the first half of the twentieth century. Her work on household production and especially the role of women dating from the 1930s, anticipates developments that have only become prominent in the past decade or so. The chapter by Alexandra Bernasek and Douglas Kinnear evaluates the pioneering contributions of Professor Allen in the microeconomics of household production and labor history.

Alton Wiley was an agricultural economist who studied the problems of rural America. One of his classic articles examined the impact of technological development on the agricultural labor supply and showed why the pace of change, when it met with institutional resistance, was particularly slow. Gerald

Vaughn provides the first comprehensive evaluation of the life and work of Wiley.

Erich Zimmermann was an internationally known authority on world resources whose famous dictum: resources are not, resources become, succinctly paraphrases the conception of resources within the institutionalist framework. Stephen McDonald sets forth the Zimmermann view of resources and how it has stood up in light of recent developments in resources, including the environmental movement.

The references at the end of the volume include extensive bibliographies of the known published and unpublished works of the six economists of the Texas School. It is hoped that this volume will enlighten those who have not previously known of the work of these economists, while at the same time providing a balanced assessment of their contributions for the many generations of economists who are their direct descendants.

Chapter 2

The Ayresian Legacy

James Ronald Stanfield and
Jacqueline Bloom Stanfield

If economic value means anything at all, its meaning is that of a gradual and continuous realization of a more effective organization of the life process.
—Clarence Edwin Ayres, 1944

Now the Welfare State is a delightful creation. As a place to live it beats anything mankind has ever known. But as an idea it leaves something to be desired. All its emphasis is on distribution and consumption ... Our ideal is—or should be—the Creative State, or the Creative Society. We favor the Welfare State because it tends to give the whole community what the whole community creates, and in doing so gives the community the greatest possible encouragement to create more, so that all of us taken together will be better off than anybody has ever been before. Thus the Welfare State is the working model of the Creative Society.
—Clarence Edwin Ayres, 1967

I. BIOGRAPHICAL SKETCH[1]

Clarence Edwin Ayres (1891-1972) was the unofficial dean of the second generation of American Institutionalists. He was born

7

May 6, 1891, in Lowell, Massachusetts, the first of three children of William S. Ayres and Emma Young Ayres. William was a Baptist minister and, before her marriage to William, Emma had been a missionary in China. Ayres's siblings, Edith and Ernest, were born in 1892 and 1895. Ceremony was an integral part of the Ayres' family life and permeated their household. Every day began and ended with prayer to a deity much feared by the Ayres children. We shall resist the temptation to speculate about Oedipal conflict in regard to Ayres's somewhat obsessive derision of ceremony and religion.

The William and Emma Ayres family also shared a passion for reading and music. This love of books and music took Clarence to Brown University in 1908 where he majored in philosophy and minored in economics. Upon graduation from Brown in 1912, he was named James Manning Scholar for distinguished excellence in college studies. After graduation, Ayres began graduate work at Harvard. He stayed at Harvard for one year, and then returned to Brown to complete his M.A. in philosophy in 1914. He left Brown not only with undergraduate and graduate degrees in philosophy but also with a wife, Anna Bryan, who was also a student at Brown. They married in 1915 and had three children before they divorced in 1925. Thereafter the children lived in Springfield, Massachusetts with their mother until her death in 1929.

Ayres studied philosophy at the University of Chicago and was awarded the Ph. D. in 1917. Immediately thereafter he was appointed Instructor of Philosophy at Chicago, a position he held until 1920. He was undoubtedly influenced by the heterodox economics department which included Thorstein Veblen, Robert Hoxie, Wesley C. Mitchell, Alvin Johnson, Walton Hamilton, and J. M. Clark. Although John Dewey had left the Chicago philosophy department in 1904, his direct influence may have lingered. Exposure to these heterodox economists may have been an important factor in Ayres's eventual shift into economics. Of course, thereafter he remained dedicated to Dewey's instrumental reasoning and its introduction into economics discourse.

Ayres remained in the academic philosophy niche for several years, undertaking a series of appointments in his early professional and academic career. After leaving Chicago in 1920, Ayres went to Amherst College as an Associate Professor of Philosophy. He resigned from Amherst in 1923, protesting what he saw as infringements on academic freedom when Alexander Meikeljohn, President of Amherst, was fired.

From Amherst, Ayres went to Reed College in Portland, Oregon, as a Professor of Philosophy. Once again, he resigned his position. This time he disagreed with administrative policies. Gwendolen Jane (Ayres' second wife) took one of Ayres' classes at Reed during the 1923-1924 academic year. From Reed, Ayres traveled east to become an Associate Editor of the *New Republic* in 1924, where he remained until moving on to an Experimental College of the University of Wisconsin in September 1925.

By then divorced and remarried, Ayres spent one year in Wisconsin, before he and Gwen moved to a ranch south of Deming, New Mexico, where they lived rent free, rather like house sitters. This carefree life changed with Anna's death in 1929. Ayres, having taken over the responsibility of raising his three children, understandably looked for work with more determination. At this juncture, his academic transition from philosophy to economics was given a strong boost by his sister Edith. She was on the economics faculty at the Washington Square branch of New York University. She secured for Ayres a summer job in that department which no doubt played some role in his receiving in the fall of 1930 an offer from the University of Texas at Austin to fill a one-year temporary Professor of Economics position The temporary position became a full-time tenured position the next year when the person on leave elected not to return to Texas. Ayres remained at the University of Texas until he unwillingly retired in 1961 at the age of 70. He continued to teach on a reduced basis until 1968 when his physician ordered him to stop teaching. In 1969, the University of Texas Board of Regents awarded him the title Professor Emeritus of Economics.

During his more than 30 year affiliation with the University of Texas, Ayres periodically took leave to fill other positions

In 1936, he served in Washington, D.C. as the Director of the Consumer's Division of the U.S. Department of Labor. From 1950 to 1953 he was a member of the Committee on the Southwest Economy. Then from 1954 to 1959 he was a director of the San Antonio Branch of the Federal Reserve Bank of Dallas.

After moving to Austin, the Ayres family customarily summered in Cloudcroft, New Mexico. There in the summer of 1972 Ayres suffered a massive stroke. On July 24, 1972, Clarence Ayres died in Alamogordo, New Mexico.

The Ayresian legacy has grown out of his philosophic background and his commitment to the progressive liberal agenda in economic policy Of his many books and papers, undoubtedly the most influential were his elucidation of the very concept of economic progress (Ayres, 1962) and his attempted prolegomenon to a mode of reasoning in economics that focused upon attainment of a reasonable society (Ayres, 1961). Perhaps most significant of all, a strong oral tradition flourished and was carried away from Austin by his many students.

II. INSTRUMENTAL REASONING

Much of the Ayresian legacy is his nurturance of the legacies of Thorstein Veblen and John Dewey, especially in regard to the Veblenian dichotomy and the philosophy of instrumental reasoning. As Ayres stressed in his own assessment of the Veblenian legacy, one must understand that institutionalists offer not simply a different mode of economic analysis but a fundamentally different view of the constitutive activities of the economy. "Veblen was trying to suggest ...a different conception of the economy itself" (Ayres 1964, p. 47). Veblen "conceived the economy as the system of related activities by which the people of any community get their living. This system embraces a body of knowledge and of skills and a stock of physical equipment; it also embraces a complex network of personal relations reinforced by custom, ritual, sentiment, and dogma" (Ayres 1964, p. 61). In Ayres's view, this conception, now known as the Veblenian dichotomy, was "Veblen's principal bequest."

One can see that this view emphasizes not the familiar buying and selling in pursuit of maximum individual gain of the orthodox legacy but rather the cluster of technological activities by which human groups derive the real income necessary for their continuity and development. To be sure this material process must be set in a more or less articulate structure of institutional constraints and motivations. Likewise the financial economy is a major portion of this configuration in the modern market economy. But this does not make calculated exchange *the* economy any more than the elaborate rituals of Medieval European fealty and sinecure exhausted the category economic.

At all times economic systems are subject to another set of regularities in addition to the nucleus of power and prestige that social status confers. This second regulatory fabric is the natural or material existence of the human species. This fundamental materiality requires a technological interaction with the rest of nature that is more or less in compliance with the regularities of natural process as understood through more or less systematic inquiry.

The critical difference in the structure of status versus the regularities of scientific understanding embodied in the unfolding state of the technologic arts is that the latter is dynamic. Science and technology are in flux, a restless state of development moved along by the inherent dynamic of the interaction of understanding with application to the practical arts of that which is understood. To be sure, some configurations of status differentiation may greatly impede the restless quest and others may substantially liberate it. The point is not that institutional or ceremonial forms are irrelevant to economic analysis, but that their relevance lies precisely in their relation to the process of inquiry and application of the insight thereby gained toward enhanced real income.

The institutional configuration does indeed embody habitual patterns of outlook and action that must be understood in order to appraise the economic prospect A *cultural* understanding of these habitual proclivities is necessary. Patterns of consumption preferences or inducements to utilize productive capacities are learned. As cultural artifacts, these behavior patters have no more or no less validity than the cultural conditioning from which they derive. For institutionalists, the question of the validity of these patterns turns not only upon the prevalent moral environment, itself culturally relative, but also upon a less relativistic concern for the impact of these patterns upon the development of the technologic process of knowing and doing. Veblen's two most celebrated works are precisely his cultural examination of the habitual outlooks that governed the patterns of consumption and enterprise behavior he observed (Veblen 1953 and 1904).

The Veblenian legacy then emphasizes necessarily an *evolutionary* focus on the economic process. The so-called dichotomy just sketched contains a relationship of tension between static configurations and notions of status and propriety and the dynamic properties of the quest to gain and apply understanding of natural regularities. Institutional or cultural lag emanates from the persistence of change of the latter complex in the face of the resistance to change of the institutional or ceremonial complex. Institutional lag causes maladjustments in the interaction of the two complexes, the system of power and status and the system of science and technology, that tends to impede the flow of real income.

In this regard Veblen stresses the difference between making goods and making money and the evolving historical context of the market capitalist economy (Veblen 1904, ch. 3). The business enterprise system in early capitalism compelled entrepreneurs to make goods in order to make money, much in the way depicted by the famous invisible hand of Adam Smith. But as the technological complex develops larger and more sophisticated methods of production, the competitive regulation of enterprise behavior is replaced by more or less concerted administration by increasingly large and powerful corporate enterprises. The business system necessarily developed the regulatory strategies of corporate capitalism to safeguard its profit margins. But this regulatory scheme is based more on retarding the production of making goods in order to secure profits than in the simple making of goods that characterized early capitalism. Making money begins to diverge increasingly from making goods.

Recognizing the economy as an evolutionary process led those influenced by Veblen, notably Walton Hamilton and Rexford Tugwell to develop ameliorative strategies. Hamilton urged that the "stream of tendencies" that comprise the economic process be viewed as opportunities to make creative responses to the challenge of enhancing the life process by exercising conscious control over the arrangements that determine the terms upon which buying and selling take place (W. Hamilton 1919; see also Stanfield 1995, ch. 1). The central focus of economic analysis in his view should be upon the mutable tendencies that can be altered in pursuit of this goal. He also noted that the corporation as a governance system is far different from the early capitalist firm and that creative interpretation and action would be required by this monumentally important institutional mutation (W. Hamilton 1957).

Tugwell also refined the so-called *concentration-and-control strategy* of institutional economics. The logic is that corporate concentration of resources and power is inevitable and it is therefore necessary to adopt a control strategy to channel this power toward the public purpose. Part of this strategy entailed public cognizance and oversight of the exercise of this power, a theme developed powerfully by J.K. Galbraith (1973a and b) as well as by Ayres, as discussed below.

The other part of Tugwell's strategy was income redistribution measures to rebalance the flows of income and expenditure in the economy. Oligopolistic industries eschew price competition and prices become downwardly rigid. Yet the technologic complex continues to develop, thereby lowering costs of production. Profit margins widen. Hence, concentration of the manufacturing sector leads to increasing skewing of incomes in the hands of those who own the equities and bonds that nominally represent the values of productive assets in this sector. Small businesses, especially retailers, farmers, and laborers experience a decline in income share

relative to those who own the financial assets of the
manufacturing sector.[2] This leads to an increase in income in
the hands of those with an orientation and the means to save
and invest. Initially the increased flow of investment seeking
income tends to inflate the values of financial assets, further
concentrating income. The bubble bursts at some point
because the underlying population lacks the purchasing
power to buy potential output at prices that validate the
nominal values attached to the productive capacity.

This is of course the ingress to the Great Depression to which
Tugwell assigned his attention as one of the New Deal Brain
Trust. In broad outline the institutionalist strategy of
rebalancing the economy was undertaken in the aftermath of
the Great Depression. Legislation and regulatory complexes
institutionalized income security programs for workers and
farmers, trade unions, small business assistance, and high
employment aggregate demand policies. Unfortunately the
other part of the strategy, control of the decisions of the
powerful, was not undertaken. The resultant inflationary bias
of the post war economy is now familiar, notably through the
works of Galbraith.

John Dewey developed one of Veblen's insights into a
philosophic outlook that was to become central to the Ayresian
legacy. With his celebrated dichotomy, Veblen distinguished
between the invidious and the non-invidious interest (Veblen 1953,
p. 143). The non-invidious or species interest is understood to be
the common good of the "generically human." The test of
"impersonal usefulness" is applied to establish that a given use
of resources is non-invidious in that it "serves directly to enhance
human life on the whole—whether it furthers the life process taken
impartially" (Veblen 1953, pp. 78-9). This direct contribution to
the "fullness of life of the individual" is drawn in contrast to the
indirect or secondary utility of goods that derives from competitive
emulation and the desire to make an invidious comparison (Veblen
1953, p. 111). The invidious interest resides in the individual's
desire to make a comparison of relative rank and status to his or
her neighbors. Veblenian waste is the expenditure of a scarce
resource to satisfy the desire for invidious comparison.

Dewey developed this insight into instrumental value theory in which the generically or non-invidiously useful is said to be instrumentally valid. A fundamental aim of instrumental reasoning is to reconstruct philosophy such that the process of inquiry and discourse that characterizes scientific communities would be extended to the realm of special values Dewey sought to convey the incompleteness and one-sidedness of the great cultural revolution that had swept through society in the modern period. Modernism was dangerously and debilitatingly immature because its experimental method had not been carried forward into the sphere of human convention and belief. The final indeed consummate significance of the great watershed of the modern scientific outlook was yet to be attained, and the way of attainment was blocked by intellectual confusion and entanglement, the removal of which could be obtained only by philosophic reconstruction (Dewey 1948, p. 52).

Dewey provided an historical overview to indicate the manner in which this systematic limitation developed, and indeed to underscore its systematic character, in order to point the way toward its transcendence by reconstruction of the habitual outlook of professional scholars and the general public. The new culture embodying the scientific outlook emerged in relation, and in substantial opposition, to the prevailing institutional configuration of the day. The two ways of knowing, through revealed authority and through the matter of facts embodied in experience, had long existed in uneasy correlative development. The gulf between them widened with accelerated development of science toward the modern period. The great reconciliation between faith and reason that supposedly ended the war between the new outlook and its animistic predecessor was less resolution than ingenious compromise. Dewey called for reconstruction to eliminate the limitations that resulted from this compromise.

The truce that allowed scientific inquiry more social space to operate involved the fundamental separation of the realms appropriate for scientific inquiry and the realms which were to remain the exclusive parvenu of vestigial authority. A series of mind-numbing dualisms emerged in consequence, the natural and the social, the secular and religious, objective and subjective, positive and normative, ends and means. At every remove such dualization proscribes and limits the reach of scientific inquiry. In Ayres's rendering, this is posed as the task of overcoming scientific separatism and the moral agnosticism that it engenders. Moral agnosticism or intellectual nihilism is an extreme relativism that holds that all values are essentially subjective and therefore lie outside the reach of scientific reasoning. But for Dewey and Ayres this was an untenable position. They maintained that the methods of inquiry, open debate, and peer review could be applied to the human task of making evaluations, and that this process is the heart and soul of democracy

For Ayres (1961), instrumental reasoning reveals that there are a handful of basic values—freedom, abundance, equality, excellence, and security—that are more or less universally held in otherwise very diverse human societies. So also is democracy, the process of collective governance that serves to advance these basic values, revealed to be a universal aspiration. But following Dewey, Ayres conceived democracy differently from the common conception of majority rule. Balloting is but the tip of the democratic iceberg. Far more important is the underlying commitment to reasoned discourse on the basis of knowledge in pursuit of the public interest. Democracy is not simply or even most importantly voting to monitor preferences and resolve preference conflicts; it is most importantly a process in which preferences are reformed with enhanced enlightenment. Democratic process is kith and kin with scientific process. The two cultures share a common commitment to inquiry. Indeed, in the instrumentalist view, the application of the process of inquiry and peer review to the social value construct implies the merger of the social scientist and social reformer in the democratic process (Tilman 1987).

III.   ON CONVENTIONAL ECONOMIC THEORY

For heterodox economists there must always be the inescapable task of criticizing orthodox price theory. Neoclassical price

theory claims to be a universal depiction of value, as applicable
to the economies of an isolated human being, a paleolithic
human band, and a command-planned communist society as
to the market capitalist economy from which it emerged. Hence
much of the heterodox task has been to indicate the
ethnocentrism of this assertion (Stanfield 1986, chs. 2, 3). The
calculative, individualistic nature of the market capitalist
economy necessarily fomented the ideology of self-interest and
competitive exchange. But earlier societies in particular lack the
institutional basis to become aware of such desiderata as
individual utility maximization in the face of relative price and
budget constraints. The charge of ethnocentrism is not labelled
solely to free anthropology and economic history from market
bias If the neoclassical depiction is not ineluctable in the past,
then neither must it be taken as eternal. Future human groups
may choose an economic culture and material organization with
different axial principles

For this reason the criticism of orthodox price theory must
also challenge its relevance, comprehensiveness, or logic for
the present economy, so to open the question of the future
economy. As noted above, Veblen challenged the identity of
making goods and making money (that is, profit) in the
aftermath of the financial consolidation that increased the
market power of large corporate enterprises. On the greatly
altered economic plane, profit-taking had become as much an
endeavor based in obstructing production as in augmenting
the flow of real income.

The relevance and comprehensiveness of a theory of value
that neglects the presence of power became a central
lamentation of institutionalism; so also have institutionalists stressed the "convenient social virtue" of their
neoclassical colleagues, who in obscuring them presence of
power serve well the interests of the powerful (Galbraith
1973b). In thus challenging the orthodox purview,
institutionalists stand alongside many generations of
socialists who demand that material organization be attuned
to human need and not to the profit of capitalists. Some
institutionalists, notable for their attention to Ayres's ideas,

have recognized this affinity and fashioned a radical interpretation of the institutionalist tradition (Dugger ed., 1989b).

Ayres's derision of the price-equals-value or making goods-equals-making money formula went somewhat further than the issue of the realism of the assumptions of perfect competition. He noted that market prices reflected not only the prevalent pattern of income and wealth distribution but mistakes in judgment and preferences for unhealthy and destructive products (Ayres 1962, pp. 226-8). The issue of course is familiar; it is that "'wants' are not primary," not somehow antecedent to the social economy. Wants "are social habits" (Ayres 1962, p. 84). Later Ayres carefully detailed the fundamental issue of acculturated wants or endogenous preferences. He argued that in the atmosphere of an individualistic culture, individual feelings took on a misplaced or fallacious concreteness. The inscrutable tastes of the individual come to have an absolute validity. Yet feelings thusly perceived are illusory for they are but the product of emotional conditioning. Human feelings are learned; human beings are socialized to respond in habitual ways to emotional stimuli (Ayres 1961, ch. 4).

The tastes or preferences held by individuals therefore have no more validity than the socialization process by which they are formed. To take them as given is to take as given that process. Much of the formation of relative prices may be seen as merely accidental and arbitrary to the logic of scarcity registered in relative prices. If people do not behave as rational calculators intent upon maximizing real income, then relative prices become arbitrary with respect to the logic of scarcity (Polanyi 1957, ch. 6; Lowe 1983, chs. 5, 6). The intervention of whim and caprice, familistic or other emotional affinities into economic decision-making leaves the resultant relative prices in a state of limbo in so far as the measurement of opportunity cost is concerned.

Perhaps of greater import, there may be a systematic thread to the socialization process from whence preferences and capacities derive They derive from the operation of social process, a process in which some individuals and groups have considerably more sway than others. Hence, to repeat, the neoclassical credulity with respect to relative prices obscures the underlying structure of power and stratification. To take as given the preferences and capacities of individuals, then to attach normative significance to the relative prices generated by these tastes and capacities, is to take as given the status quo structure of power and inequality (Stanfield 1995, ch. 1). Moreover, the orthodox ingenuousness precludes development of a critical theory of the personalities of the extant economic culture. The possibility that popular perceptions of the good life are distorted, debilitating, even dangerous, and so configured in the service of the vested interests of the powerful few, cannot even be examined (Dugger 1989c; Stanfield 1994, chs. 1, 4).

Hence, the realism of the perfectly competitive model is not the crux of the issue. Even a competitive market economy would reflect evaluations that emerge from the social process. The validity of these valuations would remain notwithstanding the perfection of the devices by which they are monitored. The conventional price theory would remain a metaphysical rationalization of a power and distributive configuration. The positivist stance of conventional economics is a sham.

When the Marxist labor theory of value is used as an axiom of *just desserts*, it too becomes a metaphysical rationalization of a given scheme of things. For as Marx himself, as well as the institutionalists insist, production is a social process ever culminating the human technological heritage any moment in this continuum is just that and no more; any theory of just desserts based productivity is mythology of prepotency, not a depiction of the concrete social process of material production.

The *scope* of conventional economics, conceived as the science of choice, largely consists of examining the allocation of givens to givens to attain the maximum real income (Stanfield 1986, ch. 2). The significant aspect of human wants is held to be their insatiability; their concrete substance need not form part of the subject matter of the discipline. Wants are taken to be infinite and given Likewise resources are axiomatically finite and their substance generally does not entertain the economic theorist; they too are given. Thusly equipped with wants and capacities to earn incomes with an eye toward want-satisfaction, the abstract human individual is the starting point of the analysis. Rationally disposed, individuals recognize the advantages of exchange; hence division of labor is generated by their rational "propensity to truck, barter, and exchange." Under certain conditions this propensity results in the maximum flow of real income possible given the resource budget constraint and the distribution of preferences and resource endowments.

This characteristic microeconomic scenario is modified in applied work and more descriptive information is utilized; but the axiomatic problematic is seldom fundamentally breached. Even the concern for macroeconomic stabilization is generally of a sufficiently short run character to reside within this framework. The focus is then to secure allocation of resources that are presently available but unused. Growth theory and the theory of technological change deal palpably with changing resources but here too the tendency is to fit the subject matter into the static maximization model of individual exchange.

For institutionalists, the problematic is different in thrust and scope. The wants of individuals and the resources available for application are part of the variables to be explained. Human wants do change and technology changes thereby redefining and remixing the menu of available resources. Wants and technology do not change randomly, nor by virtue of some natural law working without human agency; they change by virtue of influences that are endogenous to the human social system. Since the human social system is fundamentally a system of *power* and *habit*, these changes emerge from the exercise of power and habit. To the extent of their power, individuals, teleological by nature, acting alone or collectively, pursue ends that refer to their habitual inclinations by use of means that are given by these same inclinations. Inventions and innovations occur as habitual ways and means are frustrated. New wants and new means flow from these innovations.

The scope of institutional economics therefore includes wants and resources as variables, not simply the exchanges and relative prices that flow from given wants and resources. This scope summarizes the evolutionary, holistic, and instrumental facets of institutionalism and blends them into a characteristic conception of the economic problem, conceived as continuous institutional adjustment to augment the flow of real income. This focus on institutional adjustment is elaborated in the section to follow.

IV. THE ECONOMIC PROBLEM AS INSTITUTIONAL ADJUSTMENT

In the first of his two major works, Ayres sketched a path for progress in the world after the Second World War. In the foreword to the 1962 edition, he baldly defined progress as "finding out how to do things, finding out how to do more things, and finding out how to do all things better" (Ayres 1962, p. xiii). He went on to insist that progress thusly defined is irresistible and everywhere at war with the status preoccupations and habitual sensibilities of propriety. Progress occurs through new combinations of previously unrelated technical artifacts or ideas that bear fruit in their admixture. This includes not only accretion of technical materials or tools but more fundamentally the spread of knowledge about material process. Hence Ayres stressed widening participation as the key to progress. The more people who have the capacity and opportunity to engage in the material process of inquiry and development, the greater the pool from whence new combinations emerge. Not surprisingly the 1980s preoccupation with capital shortage and physical capital formation to the neglect of human capital formation is especially galling to institutionalists. Capital formation can be advanced by more and better tools if the skilled labor force is present to utilize them It can also be advanced by increase in the skilled labor force without any accretion of additional tools (Ranson 1987). No doubt much damage was done to the ability of the U.S. economy to deliver real income by the neglect of vital social programs in this woefully misguided era of Republican economics.

Ayres insisted that the problematic of economics as a social science must be evolutionary in scope and method and dedicated to institutional reform. Technology and society are viewed as continuously in flux; *the* economic problem is conceived as the continuous adjustment or reconstruction of economic institutions, in light of technological and social change, to more perfectly serve human needs and development. The economic problem thusly conceived is an adaptive process to secure continuity of existence as the basis for individual development.

Technological and social change is neither random, nor guided by some natural law external to human agency; these changes occur by virtue of influences that are endogenous to the human social system. Since the human social system is fundamentally a system of *power* and *habit,* these changes emerge from the exercise of power and habit. To the extent of their power, individuals, teleological by nature, acting alone or collectively, pursue ends that refer to their habitual inclinations by use of means that are given by these same inclinations. Inventions and innovations occur as habitual ways and means are frustrated new wants and new means flow from these innovations. Examination of the social process by which these changes occur is essential to the comprehension of the economic activities of any human group. The changes in the wants and resources and the social process from which they derive form part of the variables of institutional analysis, in contrast to their exogenous, parametric status in more conventional economics. The institutionalist problematic is then to examine these changes with an eye to their effects upon the flow of real income. Of particular concern is the process of *institutional adjustment* that these changes set in motion. Human society is holistic and interdependent; changes, especially those involving the technology by which the species necessarily reproduces itself as a set of material creatures with socialized behavioral patterns, ramify throughout the system. Technical advances raise new issues of individual behavior, law, ethics, policy, education, and so on.

Some of those with power and status may resist changes that threaten power and status; but just as surely others with power and status are likely to be maneuvering to initiate changes felt likely to result in augmentation of their relative ranks. Change is seemingly irresistible but it brings in its wake problems of maladjustment in the face of inertial ignorance or dedicated resistance from those with vested interests in potentially obsolete ways and means. Such institutional maladjustment can have dramatic consequences for the flow of real income.

The characteristic focus of institutionalist economic thought with regard to the democratic capitalist societies is institutional adjustment toward the continuous reform of the regulatory complex within which the commodity production process functions. Economic policy is part of the economic problem of socially controlling economic behavior to sustain a functioning economic order. As technological and social changes disrupt the established ways and means by which people make a living and order their existence, the key questions of the economic problem for institutionalists present themselves in terms of institutional failures and lacunae. Effective economic policy lies in mandating institutional adaptations to overcome these discontinuities. The process of identifying and implementing progressive institutional adjustment faces severe obstacles. Such change is costly in itself in that human beings are creatures of habit who evidence considerable inertia to revamping their comfortable modes of use and wont. Moreover, institutional adjustment means redistribution of power which is inevitably resisted by those who are currently well-served by the institutional configuration. Hence, considerable institutional or cultural lag will always exist in human society so that a menu of ideological re-viewing and practical reform is a permanent feature of the social landscape.

In his statement of economic progress, Ayres sketched a strategy for progress to guide the opportunity presented in the immediate post war period. The strategy consisted of intensive and extensive development of the New Deal. Domestically the principles of balancing income flows and revamping the success criteria of corporate America were to be deepened to secure universal participation in socially responsible prosperity. Advocating the concentration-and control strategy common to most institutionalists, Ayres argued that more veracity and accuracy would be needed about corporate activities to enable the democratic control by regulators and public opinion. Ayres viewed the open corporate book as the functional equivalent of a street light in the interest of public safety (Ayres 1962, pp. 252-257). *Publicity*, it must be remembered, is a primeval process of social control.

The effort to redistribute income in order to secure balance in the economy flows out of Veblen and Tugwell. Veblen's insights on the financial consolidation of industry were seen by Tugwell to have created severe imbalances in the flows of purchasing power. Given oligopolistic pricing and technical progress, the owners of the manufacturing industries gained relative to the rest of the population. Small business owners, farmers, and workers were unable to supply sufficient purchasing power to buy the goods that potentially could be produced (Stanfield forthcoming, Ch. 2). For Ayres, as for Keynes, it is necessary to institute an offset policy to counteract the fundamental tendency of finance capitalism. In the struggle to accumulate financial power, the limitation on the income and purchasing power of the masses wastefully restricts output. Creation of purchasing power by income transfers and public sector projects counteracts this tendency and rescues the potential output that would otherwise go unproduced and wasted (Ayres 1962, pp. 259-282 and 1946; see also Dillard 1987).

Of course, the macroeconomic concern is not alone. Ayres also thought that not only humanitarian concern but the desire for progress militated toward income redistribution. Progress for all would be advanced by the widening participation that income redistribution would bring about. Wider participation would magnify the opportunities for creativity and new departures in knowledge and technique. For this reason, Ayres and most institutionalists advocate some manner of guaranteed income to separate the financing of household livelihoods from its direct connection to production (Ayres 1966; see also Galbraith 1958 and 1967).

Internationally, these principles were to be applied in a World New Deal intended to promote global economic progress and head off the abysmal deprivation that foments disorder and military conflict (Ayres 1962, p. 281; see also Markowitz 1973).

Ayres was well aware that the path to progress was blocked by Veblen's obdurate nemeses, the sentimental residuals of natural property rights and nationalistic preference of sovereignty over prosperity (Ayres 1962, ch. 13). He envisioned a stark choice that the industrial democracies would exercise between reform and wider participation or authority and property: "perhaps the world will 'choose' authority rather than plenty" (Ayres 1962, p. 294). In effect he posed the question as to whether or not the industrial democracies would make the institutional adjustments necessary to reduce Veblenian waste, that is, the expenditure of scarce resources not in the service of the generic life process but to protect the privilege of the few.

The record is not encouraging, despite the unparalleled quarter of a century of sustained economic advance in the American economy. This was growth beset by a dangerous militarism and fostered by American diplomatic hegemony and corporate cultural hegemony (Bowles et al., 1983; Dugger 1989c). The seeds of institutional impasse were sown by chronic neglect of structural problems (Stanfield 1995, pt. one). The evidence suggests that Veblen's nemeses continue their sway and that Veblenian waste persists in its malevolent sabotage of the quality of human life.

V.   APPLIED ECONOMICS?

Applied economics is generally taken to mean field studies yielding policy conclusions.[3] Like others in the Texas School, Ayres engaged in such undertakings, working with the American Civil Liberties Union (ACLU) and other organizations in Texas. He also discussed policy issues in his many essays in *The New Republic* and elsewhere and held a few governmental posts as indicated above. Undoubtedly the major link between Ayres and his colleagues engaged in field work was that of philosophic principle. His economics stressed applicability to social problems, not a search for universal principles in the manner of neoclassical economics. He did not seek an economics of what was "out there" to be examined without engagement by the observer and without grounding in the relevant institutional context. Instrumental economics is applicable economics, upholding the principle that an idea is ultimately validated by its usefulness.

In the main, Ayres's policy proposals focused on the grand problem of his age, the Great Depression. In the interest of "keeping the machines running" he thought that income redistribution to sustain aggregate purchasing power was essential. This so occupied Ayres's attention that one observer has asserted that "Ayres's central analytical position is that the defects of the economy are due to the maldistribution of income, because it causes underconsumption" (Walker 1978, p. 618). No doubt the problem of aggregate stabilization at high employment was very much on Ayres's mind, so it was on the minds of his generation. But there is more to his concern with maldistribution than simply high employment. Oddly, Walker cites an article in which Ayres supports a guaranteed annual income (GAI) along these lines. After noting that boosting aggregate demand is the most immediate appeal of the GAI, Ayres goes on to say that "the most important function such an institution could perform would be to restore the reality of free private enterprise" (Ayres 1966, p. 169). He reasoned that once possessed of minimal economic security, the disadvantaged would reorient themselves within the industrial economy and become productive participants in its advance. Maldistribution obstructs participation by limiting the life chances of disadvantaged individuals and groups. This is a problem not only of humanitarian concern but an obstacle to further economic progress. Progress emerges from new combinations of previously dissimilar ideas or artifacts. The more people fully participating to the limits of their capacities in the process of tinkering, the wider the pool from whence new combinations can emerge. Hence, widening participation is supported not simply by the mores of humanitarian concern but also by the rather more objective predisposition to progress.

There seems to be no doubt that Ayres went overboard in his derision of ceremony and the ritualistic fabric of human life. He seemed to regard progress in the technologic arts with an uncritical eye, and to neglect the psycho-cultural dimension of human well-being. In his elaboration of the Ayresian tradition of instrumental reasoning, Marc Tool has indicated a key area that Ayres seems to have neglected, that being, cultural continuity. This is evident in what has become the most celebrated phrase of the postwar institutionalist lexicon: *"that way is forward which provides for the non-invidious re-creation of community through the instrumental use of knowledge"* (Tool 1979, p. 293). Modern institutionalists do not see the problem of institutional adjustment one-sidedly as overcoming the inertial resistance of institutions to technological change. Institutional preservation is also important because cultural continuity must not be rended by excessively rapid or ill-designed economic change. The unfolding life process is shaped, defined, and interpreted by a context of patterned meanings, that is, culture. These patterned meanings inculcate the individual with respect to society's systems of communication and sanctions.

It must also be said that Ayres and other institutionalists have neglected the task of explicit development of a more systematic method or procedure for instrumental reasoning. The peer review process is critical to any scientific community, and more is needed than whether or not one agrees with the conclusions of another's instrumental reasoning. Criteria for the conduct of instrumental reasoning need to be developed and tested in the laboratory of field work. These criteria need to be tested in a variety of institutional contexts in order to remain faithful to the comparative method that is the essential procedure of any institutional analysis (Stanfield 1986, ch. 2). With their methodology thusly underdeveloped and their research efforts excessively focused upon Sepulchral Studies, institutionalists have left themselves open to criticism that, at best their cause is to relax the restrictive assumptions of conventional economics and to provide a more satisfactory empirical basis for economic studies. At the worse, the cause is said to no more than destructive carping about the limitations of the conventional approach, with little or nothing by way of alternative conduct of economic investigations (Blaug 1985, pp. 708-711).

Perhaps institutionalism needs to be a *political movement* rather than simply an assembly of scholars. Allan Gruchy, many readers will remember, was a tireless advocate of that course. So also is J.K. Galbraith a monumental exemplar of the useful economist. But other institutionalists envisage a much more limited scope for instrumental reasoning and insist that advocacy of what ought to be is outside that scope (Mayhew 1987). Whether or not they should seek to develop as a political movement, it would seem that institutionalists need to offer a *political* economics which is cognizant of the political effects and objectives of economic policy, of the ways in which political processes shape economic policy and structure, of the culture of the political process, and of the effects of the economy on the polity (Hutchison 1981, ch. 2). Moreover, it would seem evident that much can be accomplished by clarifying the ongoing political discourse. In any event, it would seem that there is a need for more field work, more participant observation, more application of our talents to the issues of the day. In so doing, the procedure of instrumental reasoning must be developed; indeed, it must be revealed within the unfolding instrumental process.

So the sinews of the Ayresian legacy are not without tender areas. Nonetheless, reports of the death of institutional economics are certainly premature. While it may be less robust than we wish it to be, the Ayresian legacy is alive and well.

NOTES

1. This section relies heavily upon Breit, 1973 and 1977; Breit and Culbertson, 1976; and Eatwell, Milgate, and Newman, 1987.

2. Part of the eventual development here is the development of more systematic organization on the part of the wholesalers and retailers who buy from the manufacturers. This countervailing power as Galbraith deems it in *American Capitalism*, allows a sharing by the distribution enterprises in the profits once largely monopolized by the oligopolistic manufacturing sector.

Such a denouement appears to now be unfolding in the Japanese economy as it moves from a producer-dominated, highly regulated economy to one with a more consumerist orientation in which retailers have more freedom in relation to the manufacturing companies.

3. The authors wish to thank Anne Mayhew for a critical reading of this section, but, of course, to accept full responsibility for remaining errors.

Chapter 3

E. E. Hale on Economic Theory and the Real World

Ronnie J. Phillips

> The Commission's fear is that graduate programs may be turning out a generation with too many *idiots savants*, skilled in technique but innocent of real economic issues.
> —Commission on Graduate Education in Economics (1991)

I. INTRODUCTION

In 1991, a report by the Commission on Graduate Education in Economics, cited above, concluded that the weakness of graduate education in economics was due to the inadequate linkages between the tools economists were learning (theory and econometrics) and "real world problems" (Krueger 1991, p. 1039). There was concern that students could come to graduate school in economics from other fields and "obtain Ph.D.'s with little or no knowledge of economic problems and institutions" (Krueger 1991, p. 1040). In their summary of recommendations, the Report stated that graduate education could be improved by providing students with applications of the tools of economics to economic problems (Krueger 1991, p. 1052).

The present state of graduate education in economics would have been particularly distressing to Edward Everett Hale, who taught at The University of Texas at Austin for nearly four decades. He was an important figure in the Texas school of economics (Phillips 1976, 1989a, 1989b, 1994; Jensen n.d.). Above all else about economics, he believed that economists should be *useful*. However, the usefulness of economists should not be limited to their employers, especially in the case of academic economists, but rather the work economists do should be useful to society as a whole.

Hale was born October 24, 1893 in Hubbard, Texas and received his B.A. from the University of Texas in 1920, and an M.A. degree from the University of Wisconsin at Madison in 1923. He never completed his Ph.D. because of disagreement with his committee over his criticism of Eugen von Boehm Bawerk.[1] He was appointed to the faculty at UT in June 1923 as an assistant professor specializing in labor economics and economic theory. He was promoted to associate professor in 1926, full professor in 1936, and professor emeritus in 1962. Hale was the chairman of the department from 1929-1934 and 1939-1959. He was Labor Compliance Officer with the Dallas Office of the National Recovery Administration in 1934-35; and Director, Division of Employment of the Works Progress Administration in San Antonio in 1935-36. (Gordon, Miller, & Morgan 1975, p. 11810). He was also a labor arbitrator for many years. He died in Austin on February 3, 1975.[2]

The fact that Hale spent more time on real world problems reflected his view that economists, if they were to be useful, must do work that relates to the problems faced by people in the real world. This was his philosophy of life, and Hale practiced what he preached. Working in the real world was important for economists, Hale believed, because "a change in the institutional structure of society will cause a change in economic theory." *Economics advanced because economists tried to solve real world problems.* Though this might sound like common sense, many economists today believe that economic theory can be developed and refined outside of the constraints of the real world. For Hale, progress in economics is impeded when economists retreat to the ivory towers and develop theory for its own sake. Hale argued that the important economists were those who provided solutions to the problems facing society at a particular historical time. Thus, according to Hale, the greatest economists were Marx and Keynes, with others lagging somewhat behind. Indeed, Hale thought that many economists were apologists for the existing social order (though not intellectually dishonest), and he had consequently much less regard for their contributions. What I will do in this chapter is first present Hale's thesis on the connection between economics and the real world, I will examine that thesis for the great economists that he discussed in his courses, and then evaluate whether Hale was correct in his assessment of the history of economic thought. I will then discuss the relevance of Hale's thesis for the present day. The conclusion drawn is that Hale's main thesis is correct, but his evaluation of what makes great economists is less satisfactory because Hale himself wrote within a particular historical time period when the future of capitalism may have indeed been in doubt.

II.   HALE ON ECONOMICS AND
THE REAL WORLD

Hale was deeply influenced by his experience at Wisconsin, according to Hans Jensen, though he did not make himself a follower of John R. Commons (Jensen n.d., p. 4). Hale's interest in economics was triggered by the events of World War I. Hale had become convinced by 1917 that the war had economic origins and decided to become a serious economist.[3] However, though interested in economics, he was concerned about the relevance of much of economic theory to real world problems. He acknowledged efforts by economists to "place their knowledge usefully at the disposal and service of the manufacturer, industrial leader, business man, and legislator," however, he believed that "economics generally is yet considered too abstract, too academic, too intellectual to be of any use to the busy man of affairs" (Hale c1926, p. 1). Further, he thought that while this was true of the present state of economics, it had not always been the case:[4]

> Policies of industry, business, and legislation are worked out today with little heed to the advice and instruction of the economists. Such, of course, was not true during the time of the Classical economists, when the new "science" was hailed with delight as pointing the way out of the maze of baffling social and political problems with which men were then beset (Hale c1926, p. 1).

Why is economics of little use today in the real world? Hale pointed to the problems with the metaphysical preconceptions and formulations of economics. The problem, he wrote, was that

> economics, still laboring under the metaphysical preconceptions of the founders of the "science," continues its highly logical theorizing about the mythical world, and states the conclusions arrived at by this process of reasoning in terms of self-evident propositions of universal validity (Hale c1926, p. 2).

From the Physiocrats to John Bates Clark and Alfred Marshall, Hale continued, the "explanation of the economic activities and life of man and the economic functioning of society has been stated, not in terms of what is actually happening in the world about us, but in terms of logical deductions from consciously chosen and preconceived assumptions" (Hale c1926, pp. 2-3). The failure of economics to become scientific is due "not in the details of its theoretical structure, nor even in the conclusions which it reaches," but rather

> in the premises from which it starts its inquiry, in the point of view from which it attacks its problems, in the purpose it has had in view, in the basis on which it evaluates phenomena for that purpose, and in the ground of legitimacy to which it has appealed for proof of its formulations (Hale c1926, p. 23).[5]

What is required for economics to become less metaphysical and more scientific, that is, more relevant to real world problems? Hale answers:

The thesis maintained in this paper is that to be scientific and not metaphysical, a theory of "value" must deal, not with value, but with valuing; must aim, not at an explanation of mythical concepts, but at a description of the activity and behavior of human beings in so far as that activity and behavior is concerned with valuing things; must be stated, not in terms of logical deductions from illogical, because merely assumed premises, but in terms of summaries of and resumes of wide ranges of observed facts and phenomena. The purpose and function of a theory of "value" is not to explain the essence and substance of value and why things have it or men give it to them, but to describe the valuing process in terms of itself and furnish suggestions and a guide to administrative bodies, the courts, business men and others who are confronted with specific problems of valuing, with determining "reasonable," "just," "fair," or "adequate" values, and the like (Hale c1926, pp. 48-49).

However, Hale believed that it was not enough to merely "collect facts and insist on data," but economics must be formulated into a "close-knit body of theory" which has as its starting point the real problems facing real people. Following Commons, Hale argues that the "real" values with which people deal are "money-values, and not labor-values or pleasure-values or social values." Therefore, economic science will begin to be exact which it is quantitatively treated in terms of money values—that is, the dollar as the unit of measurement (Hale c1926, pp. 49-50). Thus early in his career, Hale stated very clearly that economics to be relevant must deal with the world as it is, and that abstract theory is of limited use, and not an appropriate starting point for useful economic analysis.

In 1933, Hale addressed a real world issue: the abandoning of the gold standard by the Roosevelt administration. Hale asks, should we be alarmed? The gold standard is yet another example of society's beliefs that turns out to be both unfounded, and its ideal operations, as conceptualized and theorized by economists, bears no relation to its real world operations. Hale writes, "It is very curious how that new invention, the gold standard, in the space of a few years, was erected into a moral principle, and how by this belief in, and acceptance of, this principle could be tested one's character as well as one's economic sanity" (Hale 1933, p. 1). As Hale then explains, the gold standard, far from being sanctioned by immemorial usage, is a recent phenomena in human history.

The economists explanation for the gold standard is that gold flows serve to settle international balances and thus keep global prices in line. However, Hale notes, it only works when there are small actual flows of gold. These conditions are met when price levels are sensitive to variations in gold reserves, the demand for international products is elastic, no tariffs or quotas, and when payments between countries are the result of the trade of goods, and not financing (Hale 1933, pp. 2-3). The mechanism has failed to work because these conditions have not been met. There is little prospect for a return to a gold standard, Hale accurately predicted. What is the alternative to a gold standard? Roosevelt had proposed a managed currency system which sought to maintain the purchasing power of the dollar, and Hale views this favorably. The gold standard was already a managed currency—managed by the bankers in their interest, and Hale thought that management by government could certainly be no worse, and quite likely better (Hale 1933, pp. 8-9). The gold standard was never a 100 percent reserve standard and the backing percentage was set by Congress, and they could change it at will.

> The choice confronting us, therefore, is not whether we shall have a managed currency, for in practice and necessarily all currencies are managed, but whether management shall be by the banking fraternity or by some other agency or group. From recent experience some of us might reasonably question the benefits of the kind of management we have had from the bankers (Hale 1933, p. 9).

With regard to the outcome of the system of managed currency, Hale believed that it would eventually mean that "Government operation of the banking system will be the logical outcome of Mr. Roosevelt's plan to establish the stabilized dollar" (Hale 1933, p. 13). The view that money causes price changes was in reality reversed: prices cause money changes. Though control of currency and credit was essential for stability, the gross inequality of income was a more important factor in reducing or eliminating cyclical fluctuations. But Hale added, "control of currency and credit is itself a necessary instrument in control of distribution of income" (Hale 1933, p. 13). It is interesting to note that right after Roosevelt's banking reforms, Hale argued that the attempt to establish a managed currency and a stabilized dollar would lead to government operation of the banking system (Hale 1933, p. 13). Thus even before the publication of Keynes's *General Theory*, Hale foresaw the enormously increased role of the government in the economy that would be necessary in the reform of the system.

Hale's belief that economics must start from the real world, and that real world problems impact economic theory were thus evident in his early writings. We can now turn to Hale's view of the history of economic thought. Hale asks the question: What makes an economist great?

III. HALE ON THE GREAT ECONOMISTS: MARX, JEVONS, MARSHALL, AND KEYNES

Economic theory must reflect the real world, in Hale's view. He thus wrote in 1949:

> Economic theory is not developed in a vacuum. Original contributions to economic thought always have resulted from the particularly pressing economic issues and problems of the time. Major problems demand solution. And the great systems of thought originally were developed in an attempt to solve problems and resolve issues (Hale 1976, p. 34).

In his lecture notes on Classical Economic Theory, Hale expressed the same view:[6]

> The theme of this course is that the development within the science of economics has been a series of responses to changing economic conditions in the economy and in society. The successful writers and thinkers are those who are concerned with the problems of their own time. They propose means for the solution of the problems in reality.... Economic ideas are the result of reality ... (Consequently, a) change in the institutional structure of society will cause a change in economic theory (cited in Jensen n.d., p. 11).

The great economists are not ivory tower theorists, interested in developing theory for its own sake, but rather those who provide solutions to the pressing economic problems of the day. Thus, according to Hale, Mercantilism grew out of the commercial revolution; Physiocracy was born of an agricultural revolution, and classical political economy developed after the Industrial Revolution. Keynes, similarly, was a result of the Great Depression of the 1930s (Jensen n.d., p. 11). Further, the great economists were *activists* who were involved in the problems of the real world, and thus had biases. Hale wrote:

> The great, i.e., well-known economists were all biased. Ricardo was a free trader because he was convinced that free trade would increase profit, which to him was essential for capital accumulation and economic development. Ricardo developed a theory supporting free trade; but he did not develop a theory he did not believe; he was not intellectually dishonest (Hale *Lecture Notes* n.d., p. 46).

This certainly applied to Marx, whom Hale considered to be the greatest economist, because his analysis of capitalism started with the real world, and Marx himself was an active participant. Hale wrote of Marx:

> Marx was a scholar, but one not solely interested in scholarly matters. He was also interested in promoting change in society. This does not necessarily follow from his dialectics, but from *facts*. The harsh facts in society are that no class in power will ever give up its position; it will hold on to its privileges (Hale *Lecture Notes* n.d., p. 14).

Marx's great contribution to economics was discovering the inherent contradiction of capitalism that the process of capital accumulation at one and the same time restricts consumer demand and increases the capacity to produce consumer goods (cited in Jensen n.d., p. 21).

Hale also did not believe that the members of the marginalist school were mere apologists for the capitalist system. In defending the marginalist school, he wrote:

I do not think that this shift to subjective theory was made primarily in order to disprove Marx; to hold this opinion would amount to believing the marginal utility theorists were intellectually dishonest. They were biased, i.e., influenced by their environment, but this is not dishonesty; dishonesty is the fabrication of a theory to support preconceived notions known to be false (Hale *Lecture Notes* n.d., p. 46).

Hale included Marshall as one of the great economists, and praised him for the connection of his theory to the real world. On Marshall Hale wrote:

To Marshall economics is the study of certain aspects of human behavior in the society in which man lives, with its social and institutional framework.... Since economics for Marshall has no function unless it throws light on problems, it certainly cannot do that unless it is fairly realistic. The economic man is too great an abstraction. A discipline which departs too much from reality becomes merely a philosophical exercise (Hale *Lecture Notes* n.d., pp. 101-2).

Interestingly, he returns to a theme from his 1926 paper for Commons, that economics must deal with matters that are measurable in money, but for Marshall this is a limitation of his theory:

Only that part of economics is scientific, according to Marshall, which deals with human motives that are measurable in terms of money, and which is able to disclose regularities in human motives that are measurable ... what would be included in economics? It limits economics to *price and distribution theory*. The core of economics for Marshall is the theory of value and distribution as it has been for orthodox economists since the time of Ricardo (Hale *Lecture Notes* n.d., p. 103).

But Marshall is clearly distinguished from the earlier orthodox economists, such as Jevons, because Marshall, according to Hale, clearly understood the historical and institutional constraints within which economics operated. Hale wrote:

There is a big difference, however; almost without exception the earlier orthodox economists had assumed the existing order to exist forever. They were aware of the fact that changes had occurred in the past, but assumed no change in the future. Now Marshall makes no such assumption. He is not only aware of the fact that institutional change will occur, hence the economic principles which he derives will have only temporary value, only within the existing institutional framework without substantial modifications. He is under no illusion that he is discovering universal laws or universal truths, as Jevons and others. Truths are valid at a given time under given circumstances (Hale *Lecture Notes* n.d., p. 104).

Jevons presents somewhat of a problem for Hale, because his thesis is that the great economists sought to solve the pressing economic problems. But what of Jevons and the marginalist school in general? Hale recognized that there was a problem with his thesis in this case. He thus acknowledged:

> It is not easy to fit the psychological theory into my thesis that economic theory is an intellectual reflection of the period in which it is developed, an intellectual reflection of the economic problems of reality. Certainly it does not fit the thesis in the sense that the theories of Smith, Ricardo and Malthus do. *Perhaps we can say that psychological economics is a reflection of the problems of the real world in a negative sort of way.* During the period of the older English classical theorists, economic problems were pressing—problems of economic policy, free trade vs. tariff, population pressures, etc. So everybody was interested in economic problems, not just professors in the departments of economics. Economics was discussed in magazines, newspapers, by men of affairs, in Parliament, all over the place. Not so after 1850-60. Then economics retired into academic halls; from 1860-1930, it was cultivated only by professors. Economics was without general interest in this period; its language and technique esoteric. Anyone who discussed economics must learn its language. What caused this development?
> There were no great economic problems demanding attention. From 1860 until about 1920 the capitalist economy enjoyed its greatest success; it embraced the world, so to speak, and operated with great success.... Economic matters were left to the learned professors in the quiet halls of the universities; and they could spin out their subtle theories in intricate mathematics, as they did not have great problems to occupy their minds.... So it was the absence of problems that, in a negative way, developed marginal utility analysis from 1860 to 1920-30. The professors had time to resolve theories incapable of solving problems because there were no problems to solve (Hale *Lecture Notes*, n.d., pp. 48-9, emphasis added).

This is an interesting variant on his main thesis. Hale contends that in the absence of pressing problems, economics is left to develop its theories in a vacuum and becomes less relevant to real world problems.

The strongest case, for Hale's direct argument, is clearly Keynes, for Hale believed that "There can be no doubt, it seems to me, that the *General Theory* resulted primarily from the momentous economic problems and issues posed by the breakdown of capitalism in the Western world between World Wars I and II" (Hale 1976, p. 34). What made Keynes a great economist? In Hale's view it is because Keynes re-discovered the inherent contradiction of capitalist accumulation that Marx had discovered, and Keynes, like Marx, sees the solution as one outside the institutional framework of a capitalist system. This, in Hale's view, is the significance of Keynes: he is Marx in sheep's clothing. Thus Hale writes of the Keynesian revolution:

> No, the Keynesian revolution does not lie in the analytical tools which he forged.... It lies rather in the *obiter dicta* which are liberally sprinkled through the book. It lies in what is easily read between the lines. It lies in the implications of the argument, in the logical import of the system as a whole. It is revolutionary precisely in the sense that Ricardo's *Principles* was revolutionary (Hale 1976, p. 39).

Hale thought that the policy prescriptions which came from Keynes would lead to socialism. Keynes failed to see the radical implications of his theories, Hale argues, because of his

> failure or refusal to recognize that he had hit upon the contradiction in the process of capital accumulation which Marx had so clearly pictured three-quarters of a century earlier. For capital accumulation is a self-limiting and a self-destructive process. The very process of accumulation destroys the profitability of further accumulation. (Hale 1976, p. 37)
> Keynes ... failed to draw the logical conclusions of his theory. These conclusions are startling, to say the least. For the reduction of the rate of interest to zero surely could not be effected short of complete nationalization or socialization of the banking system, and the banking or credit system is the very heart of capitalism (Hale 1976, p. 36).

In an eloquent statement of how Keynes unknowingly accomplished Marx's purpose, Hale wrote:

> What the bushy-bearded, heavy-handed German revolutionary did with malice aforethought and by frontal attack, the English aristocrat, a scholar of Eton and King's College, Cambridge, a director of the Bank of England, an advisor to the Chancellor of the Exchequer, a peer of the Realm, performed neatly, skillfully, and unconsciously, by flank attack (Hale 1976, p. 40).

Keynes is a great economist because he sought to solve a real world problem, he rediscovered the inherent contradiction that Marx had pointed out, and Keynes, like Marx, found the solution to the problems of capitalism outside of the institutional structure of the system. Keynes could still be classified as a great economist despite the fact that he failed to realize the real implications of his theory, according to Hale.

IV.   EVALUATING HALE'S THESIS

Hale has a main thesis and a corollary. The major thesis is that institutional change in society will change economic theory, and the corollary is that the great economists are those who start from solving real world problems. I believe Hale's major thesis is correct: economic theory is a reflection of real world problems and economic theory develops as real world problems are confronted. This view is somewhat at odds with that of economists who believe that theory can be developed on its own, for its own sake, outside the boundaries of real world constraints. In my view, those who believe in theory for theory's sake, while they may find their work personally pleasing, and possibly even publishable, are not economists in Hale's sense. The example I would use would be Gerard Debreu's response upon winning the Nobel Prize to a question about the real world relevance of his work, to which he reportedly replied: "There is none." Hale would have undoubtedly taken a dim view of giving Debreu the Nobel Prize in Economics.

There is ample evidence for Hale's thesis that a change in the institutional structure of society results in a change in economic theory. This thesis is much more than a matter of looking at the work of major economists, but rather looking at the work of the typical economist by examining published work. One only has to mention questions such as trade, unemployment, human capital, and so on, to recognize that economists have responded to real world problems, and even provided solutions to some. Economics can be of practical value. We are acutely aware of this now because of the ruckus over the appointment of Laura D'Andrea Tyson to be chair of the Council of Economic Advisors. If ever there was a wake up call to economists that they have to deal with real world issues, and provide real solutions that also take political and social factors into account, then Tyson's appointment is it. Undoubtedly, some will question Tyson's "academic" qualifications, but what is the value of the opinion of economists who refuse to modify their theories to take into account institutional constraints in the real world?

But are the great economists those who solve the big problems? I think this issue is stickier, because Hale himself was writing within a particular historical time period when capitalism was in crisis and there were alternatives existing in the world. Though Hale was not a naive socialist, there is little doubt that he believed capitalism to be doomed and he welcomed its demise. This was not to be by a Marxian revolution, but rather by a Keynesian revolution. A good example of the revolution that Hale thought would take place is the socialization of investment. Even before Keynes, Hale was discussing the tendency toward government regulation and direction of banking. Hale believed that eventually government would take over the lending activities of banks and therefore direct savings toward socially productive uses. Was Hale right? I think that undoubtedly we have seen an increasing tendency toward the socialization of lending, but it has not meant nationalization of banking, but rather government regulation and supervision. The basic institutional structure of banking has not changed, however. The profits remain private, while

increasingly, the costs are socialized. This was what the savings
and loan debacle was all about.

The case of Jevons is of particular interest, because I believe
it also has relevance for the situation in economics today. Hale
generalizes that Jevons was writing at a time when there were
no big economic problems, and thus economics could develop
on its own apart from society. I find this unconvincing because
I don't believe there was ever a long period when there were no
economic problems. Hale did not like Jevons, and did not think
that he was really a great economist, but he could not be ignored.
How to rectify this with his thesis? I don't think Hale could,
and it really raises the issue of the relevance of marginal utility
theory as a starting point and whether economics can and
should be developed for its own sake.

It is also important to remember that when Hale told his
students that all economists have biases, and that this is not bad,
he was also talking about himself. When Hale spoke of the need
for economists to be activists and involved in solving real world
problems, he was telling them what they should do, and setting
an example at the same time. Hale was an advisor to the Federal
Reserve Bank of Dallas, San Antonio branch, and a labor
arbitrator; he worked in the New Deal. He was involved in the
real world and this is what will make economists productive
members of society.

V.   CONTEMPORARY ECONOMISTS AND ECONOMICS FROM A HALIAN PERSPECTIVE

I will conclude with some speculations on how Hale might
view the current state of economics. It is tempting to say that
Hale would pick up a copy of the *American Economic
Review*, or better yet, something like the *Journal of
Economic Theory* and conclude that economists have gone
over the deep end and have finally achieved total irrelevance.
It would confirm Hale's view, as summarized by Jensen,
that:

when economists turn from the solution of real world problems to the solution of puzzles, Hale felt that their discipline is reduced to a game to be conducted for its own sake. Secondly, he was of the opinion that increasing professionalization and mathematicalization of normal economic science are synonymous with expanding intellectual conservatism which presents growing barriers to the acceptance of potentially promising new departures in economics (Jensen n.d., p. 17).

However, after further reflection, and perhaps more information about what has happened in economics, I think that Hale would find such a judgement of total irrelevance incorrect. Economists do try to solve real world problems and they do so today. The mathematics and econometrics in the articles would be foreign to Hale, but many of the titles would not be. The problem is the recognition that mathematics is a tool and it can be used by physicists, chemists, and even economists, but is subject to the limitations of mathematical logic. Given what we now know about the structure of mathematics, you can not defend the use of calculus by physicists while condemning its use by economists.

One also might be tempted to develop Hale's thesis that Jevons and marginal utility theory rose to prominence because of the absence of real world problems, and apply that to explain the present state of mainstream economics. I do not think Hale was right about Jevons's time, and I do not think it would be correct today to say that there are no economic problems.

Hale's main thesis was correct, but he was, as we all are, historically conditioned and constrained. Economics is advancing and economists are doing useful, productive work. The percentage of economists who are doing theory for theory's sake is small. There is a good reason for that because if you are a new Ph.D. trying to get tenure, publishing pure theory is quite difficult. I for one, would not conclude that the difficulty of publishing pure theory reflects its higher value, but rather it is a small part of economics because it is largely irrelevant to real world problems.

For all of the theorizing about free trade over the past two hundred years, we still want managed trade. The clever economists, and the ones who are now influencing policy, found a way to solve the dilemma of trade. The solutions have a theoretical, and mathematical basis, but they respond to the politicians and the populace that rejects the belief that all trade is welfare maximizing. We all know that the "free trade" agreement is really (and obviously) a managed trade agreement (Krugman 1990, 1994; Tyson 1993).

VI. THE NEW INSTITUTIONAL ECONOMICS

The rise of the "new institutional economics" would have greatly heartened Hale, especially, I believe, the work of Nobel recipient Douglass North (1990). In his Nobel Prize address titled "Economic Performance Through Time," Douglass North wrote:

> Neoclassical theory is simply an inappropriate tool to analyze and prescribe policies that will induce development.... (it contains) two erroneous assumptions: (i) that institutions do not matter and (ii) that time does not matter (North 1994, p. 359).

As developed by North, the new institutional economics, as applied to the problem of economic development, retains the fundamental assumption of scarcity and competition and the analytic tools of microeconomic theory, but it modifies the rationality assumption and adds the dimension of time (North 1994, p. 359).

Institutions, the humanly devised constraints that structure human interaction, are, according to North, "not necessarily or even usually created to be socially efficient; rather they, or at least the formal rules, are created to serve the interests of those with the bargaining power to create new rules" (North 1994, pp. 360-361). The interaction between institutions (the rules of the game) and organizations (created by individuals to use the institutions to their advantage) shapes the evolution of an economy (North 1994, p. 361). The fundamental problem which economist should address is the problem of institutional adjustment, because as North notes, "There is no guarantee that the beliefs and institutions that evolve through time will produce economic growth" (North 1994, p. 363).

The role of technology, so important in the analysis of the "old" institutionalists, never really fit in to the neoclassical framework, North observes. In this regard, North praises the work of Marx, and Hale would certainly share North's view that Marx's work was "a pioneering effort to integrate the limits and constraints of technology with those of human organization" (North 1990, p. 132). The basic question is what produces economic growth and improves the condition of the human race? It is a question which Hale sought to answer through his life's work, and it is a question which the new institutional economics seeks to answer within a framework which recognizes that history and institutions matter. In this regard, the work of E.E. Hale is very much in the tradition which the new institutional economics continues.

VII. CONCLUSION

There is no doubt that a good part of the profession is obsessed with technique, but these are all lesser economists. I think Hale would be pleased with what he saw in the profession today, especially as argued above, with the emergence of the new institutional economics. The development of technology, computers and new econometric techniques, are useful tools. When they are developed for their own sake as a game, they do not contribute in any useful way to the human race.

The bottom line for Hale is always: economists should use their training and tools to make the world a better place. If you stay in the ivory towers and publish theoretical articles, you are not making economics useful. Hale was a useful economist and tried to make the world a better place.

Hale was optimistic about social change, though doubting that capitalism could survive. Jensen concludes about Hale:

> I think that I may fairly postulate that he conceived of the capitalist order in the manner of a system that is so structured that it is incapable of surviving on its own power. He was confident, however, that the underlying structure could be corrected through institutional

adjustments.... Hale held the Commonesque opinion that structural
change *could* be effected through institutional engineering (Jensen n.d.,
p. 26).

Who will be the great economists of the future? It will be those
who can both explain and provide solutions to the social
upheaval wrought by rapid technological change and
institutional disintegration. Those economists in the Marx,
Veblen and Commons tradition have a head start in the endeavor
to make economics an evolutionary science.

ACKNOWLEDGMENTS

I would like to thank Wendell Gordon and Rick Tilman for supplying
copies of unpublished Hale articles and Clifton Grubbs who supplied
a copy of the transcribed notes of Hale's course on Classical Economic
Theory: Marx, Jevons, and Marshall. Jerry Vaughn supplied a copy
of a hard to find book review. I never met Hale, and I have benefitted
greatly from the work of Hans Jensen on Hale, however, any
misinterpretations or wrong views herein expressed should not be
attributed to Professor Jensen. I would also like to thank Bill Breit
who initially provoked my interest in Hale and who has supported
and encouraged my work on the Texas school over the years. Earlier
versions of this paper were prepared for the Association for
Institutional Thought meetings, April 20-23, 1994, Albuquerque, New
Mexico and the Missouri Valley Economic Association, February 23-
25, 1995, Kansas City, Missouri.

NOTES

1. A rumor which circulated around Texas for many years was that
material from Hale's dissertation research later appeared in Commons's *The
Legal Foundations of Capitalism*. The evidence is circumstantial. Another
rumor which circulated was that Hale had a manuscript prepared in the early
thirties that contained the substance of what became known as Keynesian
economics. The story goes that when the *General Theory* was published in
1936, Hale put his manuscript in a drawer and forgot about it. Unfortunately,
this story is untrue.

2.   For whatever reasons, personal as well as political, Hale published very little. There is a 1937 paper on "Fascism versus Communism" in which he predicts that if another world war or depression were to occur, "a revolution of some sort, communist, fascist, or other, probably would be inevitable in Great Britain, France, and the United States." (Hale 1937, p. 24) There is also a posthumously published paper on the implications of Keynes' *General Theory* which Hale wrote in 1949, which I will discuss shortly (Hale 1976).

3.   Jensen writes:

> When he returned to The University of Texas to resume his undergraduate studies after his discharge from the Army in 1919, Hale did so as a troubled person. He once told me that he had become convinced by that time that the First World War, and its protraction for four years, had economic causes and roots. He was therefore of the opinion that the discipline of economics might contribute to the prevention of a reenactment of the Great War. He felt so, he said, because sane policies had to be based on economic literacy as a means to the fostering of an understanding of the relationships among war, peace, politics, and economic phenomena. (Jensen n.d., p. 3).

4.   The following quotes cited as c1926 are from a paper that Hale wrote for a course taught by John R. Commons at the University of Wisconsin while Hale was a graduate student. This paper was supplied by Rick Tilman who surmised that the date was around 1926.

5.   In the paper, Hale cites Veblen's "Why Economics is not an Evolutionary Science."

6.   During the 1950s, students in Hale's economic thought classes transcribed his lectures. References here are to either the notes on Marx, Jevons, and Marshall in my possession, or to references in Jensen, n.d.

Chapter 4

Robert Montgomery:
A Gentle Iconoclast
In Industrial Organization

Robert Kling

Late in his long and impact-laden career, Robert Montgomery was invited to the University of Oklahoma to deliver a series of special lectures to eager graduate students. When they asked for a transcription of his talks, Montgomery objected that he had tried for years to develop a pared-down written summary of his essential thoughts. But, he said, he had up to that point not offered such a summary because he was afraid that anything that went beyond ten pages would provide too much fodder for "scholars" tempted to read into his words all sorts of complex meanings beyond whatever he was really trying to convey.[1]

My present mission is to summarize and assess Robert Montgomery's contributions to economic thinking, economic policy-making, and economic education—to the "Texas School" of economics and to industrial organization economics specifically. In doing so, I hope I will not violate Montgomery's desire to be taken as a down-to-earth economist with a few straightforward powerful messages about economic culture

51

and economic policy. I hope I will be able to analyze and synthesize his work without overinterpreting it. And I hope I can present the core of Montgomery's intellectual contribution without slighting the immense impact he had as a personality.

I.   A BRIEF BIOGRAPHY

Robert Montgomery served on the faculty of the Economics Department of The University of Texas at Austin for over four decades, and played a key role in defining the "Texas School" of economics.[2] Born on January 9, 1893, in Blanco County Texas as the tenth of twelve children of a circuit-riding frontier minister, the young Montgomery pursued his high school and college educations while living with kin in San Marcos. Serving for a time as local high school science and math teacher, and then as a much envied Army aviator during World War I, Montgomery continued his education at the University of Kansas, where he earned his B.A. degree in 1921 and where he taught the year following. Moving on, he gained his M.A. degree from the University of Texas in 1923, and the Ph.D. from the Robert Brookings Graduate School in 1926. Montgomery served on the faculty at the University of Texas until his retirement in 1963, taking occasional leave to teach at the University of Pennsylvania and the University of Pittsburgh, to serve his country during the Depression (with the Federal Planning Division, the National Resources Committee and the Agricultural Adjustment Administration) and during World War II (as Chief of the Economic Objectives Division, Board of Economic Warfare, and as Economic Advisor to the Director of the Foreign Economic Administration). Montgomery spent 15 years of retirement in San Marcos, until his death on June 6, 1978.

How did Bob Montgomery evolve as an economist during these years? Maurice Erickson gives a summary portrayal:

> Dr. Montgomery's early academic interests were in mathematics and
> science, interests he retained throughout his life. But as he grew

older, he became increasingly attracted to the study of the vast social and economic changes that were evolving from the frontier society he had experienced as a youth. This effort to study and understand the forces of change and to pass his ideas and thoughts to others who he hoped might join the crusade, became the prevailing passion of his life. With this passion, and with his unique talent for teaching, he undoubtedly influenced thousands—students in his classes, and audiences of innumerable lectures he gave throughout the country. (Erickson n.d., p. 2.)

Actually, it was while he was at the University of Kansas as an undergraduate that Montgomery was first exposed to Institutionalism—in the classes of KU's legendary John Ise, who made a habit of offering students large doses of Thorstein Veblen. Then as a student in Austin, the budding scholar would have encountered the influences of a cadre of thinkers who over the years evolved into the "Texas School", and whom Montgomery would soon join as a faculty colleague.

Throughout his career, Montgomery's writings focused on the efficacy of market institutions in meeting social needs, and thus on the merits of social versus private control of markets. Within this broad theme, Montgomery's work took several turns. He began by addressing the failures of competition in agricultural markets; he followed by taking up issues of unregulated monopoly in resource markets and of regulated monopoly in utility industries; in the long tail of his career he focused more and more on the "big picture", on the long sweep of history and the anthropological bases for economic organization, on the forces of change and the barriers to change.

For Robert Montgomery, the role of economics was to assist in the development of relevant social policy. Whenever he was expounding new and important theoretical ideas, he did not fail to explain them in terms of their applications to practical matters. And he did not limit his deliberations to armchair philosophizing: he took an active role in policy formulation at both the local and national levels. And certainly, one of Dr. Bob's greatest contributions was as a master teacher who inspired a generation of students to question the *status quo*, to consider the social interest and to pursue careers in

Institutional economics. In this way as in the others, Montgomery established his place in what has become known as the Texas School of Economics.

In this chapter I choose to focus on Montgomery's scholarly contributions in several areas of industrial organization: problems with competition, problems with monopoly, and proposals for sensible public utility regulation. However, I shall also summarize other aspects of his work that characterize Montgomery the "whole" economist: his contributions to the formulation of public policy, to the formation of economic understanding via his teaching, and to the establishment of the Texas School.

II. PROBLEMS WITH COMPETITION

Through the 1920s, Montgomery's work was dominated by analyses of the cotton market and the cooperative movement. Anchored by his doctoral dissertation, "Present Status of Law on Cooperative Marketing Associations", and showcased by his 1929 book, *The Cooperative Pattern in Cotton*, this literature presents an analysis of the failure of *laissez-faire* in cotton farming and of the spread of the cooperative movement in Texas. In the book, he presented a strong case against the desirability of the traditional marketing system, and supported the case with evidence from three market studies done between 1912 and 1919.

Much of Montgomery's critique focused on problems of incomplete information. Decrying the "great injustices" caused by geographically nonuniform prices, he stressed the "continuous and complete failure of competition in securing a fair price to the farmer for his cotton." The only possible conclusion, he said, was that

> ... competition is not, after all, the precise, definite, shrewdly calculating, and eternally just regulator of prices that we have been wont to consider it. At least not in this specific case. (Montgomery 1929, p. 40.)

Arbitrage was not playing its role. Prices were not only inconsistent across space but also highly variable over time; the result was enormously unstable farm incomes and the attendant problems.

A related information issue addressed by Montgomery was that of quality and of the need for a high level of information regarding the grade of cotton traded. Citing evidence of overly discounted prices for lower grades and insufficient premiums for higher grades, he emphasized the enormous advantage to the farmer of knowing the grade of his product. In various respects Montgomery was an early analyst of market failures grounded in lack of information.

Farmer incomes suffered not only because of information problems but also, according to Montgomery, because of an unfortunate interaction between technical improvements on the one hand and farmer immobility on the other. Improved production methods adopted by progressive farmers resulted only in plunging prices, since in this market the less efficient producers were not driven out:

> Their equipment, their farms, and their whole life and training keep them growing cotton when this undoubtedly means a life of consistently declining standards. Unfortunately there are no bankruptcy courts to liquidate the assets and close out the businesses of patently failing cotton farmers. (Montgomery 1929, p. 259)

In the cotton market, according to Montgomery, it was not that competition failed to exist, but that it failed to perform correctly. "The present organization fails notoriously in the first prerequisite of any industrial organization, namely, in providing an acceptable standard of living for the people engaged in the industry" (Montgomery 1929, p. 250). "Can Free Competition, in the generally accepted meaning of the term, solve the problem? It has had somewhat over a century in which to work its magic—and here we are!" (Montgomery 1929, p. 253). As an alternative, Montgomery called for expansion of the role of cooperatives:

> The first thing the cotton farmer must do is to give up a measure of his religiously treasured and dearly bought independence. To go back to a self-sufficient frontier agriculture is impossible. To retain the present industrial anarchy in a closely coordinated, highly centralized, large-scale economic order, is downright folly. The only thing he can do is to assume the responsibility of consciously organizing his industry with the purpose of regulating production and price ...
>
> The one agency in existence today that can handle this program is the large-scale cooperative. (Montgomery 1929, pp. 262-263).

The cooperative's mission, he wrote, must include "the function of determining the price policy for the whole industry, and of promulgating a production program in harmony with it" (Montgomery 1929, p. 264). Montgomery did not make this proposal lightly; he outlined the problems to be faced, including the organizational challenge of recruiting good leaders, and the strategy challenge of setting the right price. In this latter regard, Montgomery offered an eye-opening analysis of limit pricing applied to agriculture:

> The case of cotton is more difficult [than the case of milk and other markets]. If the price is set too high for a number of years and other competing areas are allowed to be brought into production, it will be more difficult to drive them from the field. This fact would have to be kept constantly in mind by the board, to offset the persistent demand for higher prices from the membership (Montgomery 1929, p. 269).

In this single short passage Montgomery offers not only an application of limit pricing to agriculture, but also a recognition of sunk costs, capacity commitments, and barriers to exit. In these areas he anticipated theoretical developments that did not come into their own until 20 years later.[3]

Indeed, a fascinating aspect of all Montgomery's studies of the cotton market is the degree to which they show him integrating his knowledge both as an agricultural economist and as an industrial organization economist. Though he turned from agriculture to address other issues in the 1930s and beyond, we ought not to forget his role as a rural Texan deeply involved in issues of equity for agricultural producers.

III. PROBLEMS WITH MONOPOLY

In the 1930s Robert Montgomery's interest turned from the failures of competition to the challenges of monopoly. He offered a string of articles on public utility regulation, and the decade culminated with publication of *The Brimstone Game*, his 1940 capstone work on monopoly in the sulfur market. In the post-war years, Montgomery continued in the industrial organization field, but mostly as a witness in front of the Civil Aeronautics Board on behalf of airlines, and no academic publications came forth.

Let us put aside for the moment Montgomery's work on public utility regulation in the 1930s, and consider his 1940 capstone work *The Brimstone Game*, which offers a captivating journey into the world of the sulphur industry. Though there are points of commonality in Montgomery's treatments of the cases of cotton and sulphur (commonality we shall discuss shortly), we cannot escape the obvious contrast. In one case, Montgomery argues against free competition and in favor of collective producer measures to raise prices and guarantee higher incomes. In the other, he paints the organizers of just such an effort as villains of the highest rank!

But there is really no inconsistency. First, it fit Montgomery's nature and the Institutionalist perspective to consider each case on its own merits and to eschew blanket prescriptions for or against competitive markets. He was most interested in pragmatic solutions to social problems. Though he villainized the sulphur monopolists for the sake of a story, he also asserted:

> What has been said heretofore, and what is to be said hereafter, is not in any sense intended as a moral condemnation of monopolists, nor of monopoly. It isn't a question of right and wrong. It is a question of an economic system that will function to give us, in a continuous stream, the goods and services we want (Montgomery 1940, p. 33).

Second, Montgomery was a rural Texas patriot, and the positions he took on cotton and on sulphur fit the interests with which he identified. The everyday Texas cotton farmer, whose plight Montgomery decried so effectively in the 1929 book, is the fertilizer buyer depicted as a major victim of the sulphur monopoly in the 1940 book. And the brimstone producers suffer his scorn all the more because they were controlled by the Eastern financial establishment, the "House of Morgan", foreigners to Texas:

> As a matter of fact, the official directories of Texas Gulf and Freeport ... boast a Rockefeller, a Rogers, a Stillman, a Baruch, a Lamont, and two Whitneys. They also show a Goodrich, a Webster ... there isn't a Texan on either board. Texas only furnishes the brimstone! (Montgomery 1940, pp. 65-66).

And so Montgomery offers his narrative of the sulphur industry as an indictment of monopoly on several counts. In a style that also characterized his teaching, he enhanced the story by a curious intertwining of the actual case study with three metaphors: the 1602 playing card monopoly case of *Allen v. Darcy*, a bronze-versus-flint fable of the stone age, and the play of a good Texas poker game. Storytelling aside, Montgomery's condemnation of monopoly reflected the difficult economic times in which he was writing, embodied his enduring interest in the role of technology in shaping society, and in some ways anticipated later developments in the field of industrial organization.

Robert Montgomery was in touch with the pressing economic issues of his day, and some of the prevailing explanations offered. In the opening chapters where he offered background motivation for his brimstone case study, he expressed the strong view that monopoly was responsible for all unemployment. Paraphrasing Thomas Jefferson, Montgomery wrote: "Where there are uncultivated lands, idle capital, unused techniques, and unemployed workmen, it is clear that monopoly is abroad in the land" (Montgomery 1940, p. 37). And in his conclusion he expounded, "The brimstone monopoly is not responsible for all unemployment—but *monopoly* is!" (p. 84). And he extended the analysis of monopoly as cause of unemployment to monopoly as cause of gluts, starting with a tale of agricultural goods and moving to the reality of the Great Depression:

... if some group owns all the good cornland, or all the corn planters, or has an exclusive royal patent on growing corn, what are the wheat farmers to do? The price of wheat may go down ever so low—the price of corn go up ever so high—and the profits of corn growing be ever so alluring, but they cannot shift from wheat to corn. The results are huge profits in corn growing and huge surpluses of wheat!

Well, that is what we have. Not in wheat and corn, to be sure, but in scores of other industries. Too much cotton and wheat and corn; too little steel and gasoline and glass and aluminum and electricity (Montgomery 1940, pp. 30-31).

Montgomery supported this line of analysis by invoking the administered price hypothesis most often associated with the name of Gardiner Means. Offering data for twenty industries to make his point, he suggested:

... some business groups had learned how to control the output of their industries. Instead of producing to capacity and then selling for whatever the market would pay, they set their prices, and produced the amount the market would take *at that price.*

That isn't the way business groups are supposed to act in a system of free competition. And it isn't the way they do act if there *is* free competition (Montgomery 1940, pp. 33).

And Montgomery even brought into his story a bit of Keynesianism: a kind of multiplier effect. Referring to his sixteenth-century card monopoly example, he wrote:

Mr. Darcy did not employ many workmen in making playing cards. But his sabotage of production affected the jobs of many others employed in the making of ink and cardboard and engraving equipment and card tables and poker chips and decanters and IOUs and swords and pistols and all the other ancillary paraphernalia used in connection with playing cards (Montgomery 1940, p. 83).

Applying the concept to the brimstone case, he enumerated the various suppliers of the brimstone industry that would expand if monopoly could be eliminated, and then pointed out that

(m)ore important and more far-reaching, each of the scores of hundreds of industries dependent upon sulphur would employ a few—or a great many—more workmen. This, in turn, would call for more barbers, beauticians, ball players, movie operators, lawyers, doctors, dentists, preachers, and teachers—plus more farmers to provide all of them with food and clothing (Montgomery 1940, p. 84).

Beyond the specific issues of the Great Depression, Robert Montgomery was interested in how the evolution of technology contributed to the evolution of society. In *The Brimstone Game* he argues that one of the "disastrous effects" of monopoly is that

... the monopolist sooner or later finds it necessary to block the introduction of new ideas and new techniques in his industry. The "morgue" has become one of the common and one of the most dangerous monopoly devices of our time (Montgomery 1940, p. 28).

Yet at the same time he notes the regularity with which new technique ultimately defeats monopoly. Here he employed his allegorical tale of prehistory.

So, the bronze ax came to Flintland—and the Beaters of Bronze replaced the Ancient and Honorable Order of Flint Workers. They in turn, monopolized their skill and the sources of their bronze; built up a system of laws and customs and business practices that gave *them* the positions of honor and power and profit—until they, in turn, faced the irresistible logic of iron (Montgomery 1940, p. 29).

Though Montgomery's deep-running interest in the tension between technology and institutions is part of what helps define him as an Institutionalist out of the mainstream, he also participated in the general evolution of mainstream theory in the area of industrial organization. Would we push Montgomery's sensibilities too far if we suggested that, in choosing the poker game as the metaphor for monopolistic strategizing in the sulphur industry, he was anticipating the widespread application of game theory to industrial organization issues such as entry deterrence and price punishment? Probably. But his discussion of the sale of monopoly franchises certainly shows appreciation for what in time came to be called the theory of regulation, and in his closing paragraphs he decries what he calls

> ... the most vital statistic of our age: the amount of intelligence and energy we are employing in formulating and manipulating devices for restricting production. If only that intelligence and energy could be employed in producing potatoes, there would be food for everybody! (Montgomery 1940, p. 93).

This appreciation of the wastefulness of rent-seeking activity pre-dates by far the oft-cited "seminal" work of Gordon Tullock (Tullock 1967).

In further discussion of how industrial organization is perverted to the service of special interests, Montgomery reveals how the directorships of the sulphur companies overlap with the directorships of major national financial and industrial powers:

> "Metal mining is represented twenty-six times; utilities and railroads, twenty-one; banks and insurance companies, seventeen; oil, eleven ... One brimstone director holds twenty other official positions, touching possibly one-fourth the corporate wealth of America. Two others hold thirteen connections each. One holds ten; two hold seven; three, six ... " (Montgomery 1940, p. 66).

The links include overlaps between the superficially rivalrous Morgan and Mellon groups; the stakes, Montgomery claims, are great enough to "reconcile the Capulets and the Montagues" (Montgomery 1940, p. 65). Indeed, these passages seem to foreshadow the "planning tableau" suggested by John Munkirs in the 1980s (Munkirs 1983).

In both *The Cooperative Pattern in Cotton* and in *The Brimstone Game*, Robert Montgomery showed himself to be a creative thinker who articulated countless ideas that others, in Institutionalism and in the mainstream, later developed into significant theories.

IV.   POINTS OF COMMONALITY

There are points of commonality between Montgomery's two
books, points that give us a bit of insight into the essence of
Robert Montgomery. First, each book offers its lessons via an
intensely thorough case study. Montgomery developed for
himself, and then communicated to his readers, an intimate
knowledge of the markets he studied. No detail was left
unexamined, no quirk unexplored. Part of the Institutionalist
tradition, this case study approach ensures that the analysis
has real-world relevance, and that behavioral generalizations
are not taken out of their institutional context. In Montgomery's case, the approach also allows him to apply his skills
as master storyteller; especially in *The Brimstone Game*, the
economic facts come alive as industrial entities become
personalities playing out a drama of market domination. Even
in *The Cooperative Pattern in Cotton*, one reads spell-bound
as he recounts the specific stories of certain farms, of certain
town markets, of certain cooperative experiences ... as he
characterizes the Cotton Belt farmer not as a faceless economic
agent, but as a human being with real personal motivations
and limitations.

Second, both books suggest a mild respect for what free
competitive markets might accomplish in the ideal. In *The
Cooperative Pattern in Cotton* this respect seems nearly tongue-
in-cheek. Montgomery says of the cotton market, "Here, if
anywhere in the world of today, we should expect to find all
those advantages which inhere in a competitive system"
(Montgomery 1929, p. 9). Then he enumerates the positive
results to be expected from competition, but adds sardonically,
"These are the conclusions derivable from the dogma of the
economic philosophy of the past century" (Montgomery 1929,
p. 10). And the rest of the book shows that, whatever
Montgomery's confidence in competitive markets, he had been
forced to suspend it for the case of cotton.

The Brimstone Game offers a lengthier, later and perhaps
more sincere treatment, including the following passages:

(O)ur forefathers ... were practicing democracy and *laissez faire.* Jefferson and Adam Smith were writing the arguments. Those arguments are not hard to understand: Leave every man alone to do as he pleases, with only such restrictions as are necessary to prevent him from despoiling his neighbors by fraud or violence ... In order to prosper he must use his energy, his intelligence and his skill in producing the things his community wants ...

Furthermore, this system will ensure the very best use of all resources, both natural and human ...

Finally, the system will be self-regulating. If too many shoes are made, the price of shoes will drop. The least skillful shoemaker will find it more profitable to raise cotton, or to teach school. If there are not enough grist mills, the price of flour will rise—and someone else will build a mill. Thus the community will have the right number of shoemakers, schoolteachers, and grist mills....

Free prices are the governor of the engine.... If it becomes impossible, or even unduly difficult, for men to get into, or out of, some industries, the proper adjustments will not be made.... That is what has come to pass (Montgomery 1940, pp. 20-22).

There is no escaping the esteem Montgomery shows here for competitive markets and the power of free prices. Time and again he calls for the protection of "free business enterprise." The message of the whole book is that monopoly is to be condemned because it corrupts the beneficial tendencies of unhampered competitive markets.

The last passage cited, and particularly this second time we have noted a reference to Jefferson, raises a third theme common to Montgomery's two books: his conviction that effective democracy requires appropriate economic institutions. In *The Cooperative Pattern in Cotton* the issue is implicit in Montgomery's impassioned plea for reasonable and stable standards of living for growers. In *The Brimstone Game* he states it more bluntly:

If we want a system of free business enterprise and a democratic government, we cannot allow the Darcys to monopolize our most important industries. As David Cushman Coyle has stated the case: 'The price of free men is free prices.'...Unless prices are free to move, our system of competitive business enterprise is at an end. And it may carry democracy down with it (Montgomery 1940, p. 25).

Montgomery cited Thomas Jefferson frequently in this book; he seems to have been a real adherent to Jeffersonian philosophy. In a particularly interesting section, he reminds us that Jefferson said jobs are a *Natural Right*, that unemployment is the result of property laws extended so far as to violate human rights. Montgomery saw the American sanction of monopoly as the modern version of a "royal grant of special privilege", that is, in the category of undemocratic institutions to which Jefferson was referring.

In fact, Montgomery makes such frequent pejorative reference to "royal grants of special privilege" and "royal patents" that one comes away with the impression of a virulent anti-royalist. Probably, he was employing a tactic that would shake his patriotic American readers out of a narrow acceptance of local landscape as normal, and spur them to entertain the notion that some familiar institutions should be recognized for what they were and how they affected society. He claimed it was the "greatest tragedy in the long history of man" that popular sentiment tended to accept corruptive power as the norm (Montgomery 1940, p. 89). In a gentle way, he was inviting readers to join him in rejecting such traditions and in looking for something better.

V.   PROPOSALS FOR SENSIBLE PUBLIC UTILITY REGULATION

In the 1930s, Montgomery published a number of articles in the theory of public utility pricing which were startlingly innovative at the time. Remarkably, despite several decades of writings in the interim, much of their content is no less relevant today. Some of his most interesting ideas appear in the two articles he contributed to *The Annals of the American Academy of Political and Social Sciences,* in an issue devoted to policies toward the railroad and electric industries. More than a half-century ago, Montgomery proposed that: (1) Utility rates should be set at marginal cost to maximize social welfare; (2) the covering of all costs, including a "fair return" on investment, should not be the paramount concern of rate-setters; (3) plant size should be expanded as long as it leads to lower average cost; and (4) the incentive a firm has to invest in cost-saving technology is inversely related to its capital-cost/operating-cost ratio. All of these arguments led him to advocate public ownership of the railroads and electric utilities.

It is interesting to evaluate Montgomery's propositions in the light of the modern regulatory literature, and *vis* [b] *vis* the experience of American utilities. Some of his ideas, notably marginal cost pricing, have been broadly adopted; others, such as his fundamental commitment to public ownership, have been passed by. Let us briefly summarize each proposition in turn.

1.   Utility rates should be set at marginal cost to maximize social welfare

Montgomery's article on "Government Ownership and Operation of the Railroads" provides a clear and convincing argument for marginal cost pricing (Montgomery 1939b). As he put it, "Production should be expanded to the point where incremental cost and demand price coincide....(P)rices should be determined by the intersection of incremental cost and the demand schedule" (Montgomery 1939b, pp. 139, 144). This idea was new at the time, and Montgomery justified it principally by providing an illustration of cost and demand schedules he claimed to be representative of the railroad industry. Using consumer surplus and ultimately total surplus as measures of welfare, he showed that the marginal cost solution yielded social gains relative to the orthodox average cost pricing method and, further, that "the net community advantage (consumer gains, less railroad losses) would be greater at this point than at any other" (Montgomery 1939b, p. 141).

To say that marginal cost pricing has become a cornerstone of regulatory policy is to drastically understate the importance it has gained in regulatory philosophy. Post-World War II mainstream economics, with its emphasis on efficiency in resource allocation, has adopted marginal cost pricing as a nearly ritualistic policy prescription. Within two decades of

Montgomery's nearly revolutionary advocation of the approach it had become standard fair. In a famous 1955 article, William Vickrey wrote, "...marginal cost must play a major and even a dominant role in the elaboration of any scheme of rates or prices that seriously pretends to have as a major motive the efficient utilization of available resources and facilities" (Vickery 1955, p. 605). The well-known regulatory economist Alfred Kahn, in his classic text on regulatory principles, writes, "The central prescription of microeconomics is the equation of price and marginal cost. If economic theory is to have any relevance to public utility pricing, that is the point at which inquiry must begin" (Kahn 1988, p. 65). Indeed, any modern economics textbook, even at the introductory level, stresses the role of marginal costs if it mentions price regulation at all.

We now recognize Robert Montgomery as an early promoter of marginal cost pricing. His writing on the topic is contemporaneous with the oft-cited work of Harold Hotelling (Hotelling 1938). In a treatise on the topic, B. P. Beckwith wrote:

> In sum, Montgomery was a pioneer proponent, perhaps even an original codiscoverer of the new theory of marginal-cost price-output control, he understood its meaning and importance, he defended it forcefully and logically, and his discussion of the theory supplements earlier discussions in significant ways (Beckwith 1955, p. 92).

Beckwith faulted Montgomery for examining the *total* magnitudes of costs and benefits in what ought to have been a *marginalist* analysis. However, this criticism is unfounded, and in fact shows an all-too-common bias that has developed, a bias toward analysis exclusively in marginal terms, when totalities may be not only instructive but indeed crucial to the accurate evaluation of an outcome or of a policy approach.

Incremental cost philosophy is in many ways responsible for the restructuring and regulatory changes that have been instituted in the telephone, natural gas, and railroad industries, among others. One particular change in regulatory practice, the abandonment of "system averaging" of costs, has been claimed by Douglas Jones to be largely a result of "the persistent attack by much of the current generation of academic economists" on the concept, an attack no doubt inspired by their attachment to marginal cost pricing as advocated by Montgomery (Jones 1988).

2. Covering of all costs, including a "fair return" on investment, should not be the paramount concern of rate-setters

Montgomery began his railroad article by attacking the commonly accepted notion that a railroad's revenue ought to cover all its costs. Citing explicit statements to that effect by Emory Johnson and Frank Taussig, he summarized, "In short, it is all but universally agreed that railroads, whether under private or public ownership, should pay their own way. I believe the opposite is true." And he proceeded to quote Alfred Marshall and A. C. Pigou on the merits of subsidizing decreasing cost industries (Montgomery 1939b, pp. 137-139).

After presenting his case for marginal cost price and output determination, outlined above, Montgomery explained that this socially advantageous approach nonetheless would lead to a deficit for the railroad, a natural consequence of average cost exceeding marginal cost. However, he also showed by illustration that the gains to society outweigh the loss to the railroad. Indeed, he went on to present the following proposition, a somewhat shocking statement but a natural corollary to marginal cost pricing: "Under conditions of decreasing cost and elastic demand if the [firm's] plant can now be operated at a profit, at capacity output, it should be enlarged" (Montgomery 1939b, p. 142). His final conclusion: "Railroads ... should be run at a loss" (Montgomery 1939b, p. 144).

What Montgomery saw as a preoccupation with allowing a fair return has not lessened in the course of five decades. Valuing the rate base, determining a fair return, and then setting rates accordingly remains the core procedure in utility regulation. It has, however, been creatively combined with the goal of instituting incremental cost pricing in many areas. Montgomery himself was perhaps the first to note that using "ready-to-serve"

charges might enable a utility to apply marginal cost pricing
but avoid revenue deficiency (Montgomery 1939a, p. 48).[4]

But Montgomery was uncomfortable with the "fair return"
requirement at another level, and this is the focus of his 1931
piece attacking the *Smyth v. Ames* decision and the chaos of
judicial directives that ensued. For practical purposes,
Montgomery supported subsidies for decreasing cost industries,
to allow them to operate at optimal levels without incurring
deficits. The legal requirement, on the other hand, that a "fair
return" be paid on the "fair value" of the rate base, seemed to
Montgomery to be an empty and counterproductive exercise,
indeed a "puerile and nugatory mental somersault" (Montgomery 1931, p. 232). He pointed out that an asset's return is what
determines its value, and to pretend to assess the two
independently was impossible. He also argued that the absence
of competition in utility markets makes the use and value of
utility investment different, and that competitive standards of
value and return should not be applied. On these points,
Montgomery was joining other institutionalist critics of the
reigning regulatory policy of the time.[5]

However, the imperative to make utility revenues cover costs,
including fair return, continues to the present day. The 1944
landmark *Hope Natural Gas Co.* decision reinforced the legal
principle, and Jones classifies "fair rate of return" as a definite
"survivor" among regulatory propositions. Indeed, such
instances of public subsidization of deficits as remain, for
example in passenger transportation, are under constant attack.

3. Plant size should be expanded as long as it leads to lower average cost

Montgomery's advocation of marginal cost pricing had led
him to espouse deficits in railroad operations; the issue of
deficits led him in turn to consider the question of optimal plant
size. Montgomery was aware of the view that inability to operate
where marginal cost at least equals average cost indicates an
inappropriately large size of plant. He had countered by arguing
that, with declining *long-run* costs, profitability was a signal

of an inappropriately *small* plant size: "The plant should be expanded as long as the output which would be taken at incremental cost can be produced at lower average cost" (Montgomery 1939b, p. 143).

Given the structure of modern microeconomic theory, there is ambiguity in the interpretation of Montgomery's plant size proposition. On one hand, we might interpret Montgomery's words as an attempt to restate the optimality of marginal cost price and output determination in terms of plant size. If that was his attempt, he erred in a way that is so obvious, within the logic of his own analysis, that it is difficult to believe he would not have seen the problem. For, understood this way, Montgomery would appear to be claiming that the firm's scale of operations should be expanded until the minimum point of the long-run average cost curve is reached. Clearly that is inconsistent with his argument that the appropriate scale of production is where marginal cost intersects demand.

On the other hand, he might be read as saying that, *for a given output level,* plant size should be expanded so long as it lowers average total cost. Using this interpretation, we might consider Montgomery to have been making an application of the envelope property of cost curves that had been expounded just a few years earlier by Jacob Viner (Viner 1931). In this case, we have an example of the way in which Montgomery unfailingly transformed esoteric theoretical concepts into practical prescriptions with important policy implications.

4. The incentive a firm has to invest in cost-saving technology is inversely related to its capital-cost/operating-cost ratio

It is in his companion article "Government Ownership and Operation of the Electric Industry" that Montgomery introduced this fourth proposition. Here Montgomery wanted to challenge the argument that private utilities would be more effective than government in instituting improved production techniques. Proceeding once again with a number of numerical examples as well as conceptual argument, he showed that, "When savings on operating costs are greater than additional capital costs (bond payments or annual depreciation, and interest charges) on new equipment, it will pay the company to install it" (Montgomery 1939a, p. 49). Montgomery carried this idea to still another conclusion, the proposition as it has been restated above.

Montgomery used this hypothesis to argue first that a purely profit-oriented private utility would have less incentive to apply new techniques than a welfare-oriented public utility. He also claimed that marginal cost pricing, rather than fair-return average cost pricing, would increase the utility's incentive to pursue such improvements. Harry Trebing has offered the following comment:

> I believe that Montgomery's most potentially significant contribution lay in his analysis of the tendency of capital intensive industries to avoid innovative investment...It might be desirable to differentiate between Montgomery's discussion of capital intensity inhibiting progressive investment and the more widely recognized Averch-Johnson effect. The A-J effect assumes a propensity toward excessive capital investment whenever the allowed rate of return is greater than the cost of capital. I think Montgomery's concept is far more significant. In fact, Montgomery's criticism of a regulator's preoccupation with total revenue requirements might be interpreted as an early recognition of the pitfalls associated with the A-J effect...[6]

Yet, of all Montgomery's propositions discussed here, this is perhaps the only one that has been really left by the wayside in the decades since his writing. Some informal observations about instances of the tendency Montgomery postulated are of interest. The steel and automobile industries in the United States are notable both for their high capital-intensity and their lethargy in instituting cost-competitive technology. Another example is in the electrification of railroads, where the United States industry lies decades behind European state monopolies in moving to what, in many instances at least, is a more progressive, less costly technology. Finally, one notable study of this issue was offered by Frederick Scherer, who examined AT&T's sluggish innovation in microwave technology.[7] We might well take more profit from Montgomery's insights in this area, as we have in others.

VI. MONTGOMERY THE WHOLE ECONOMIST

Though this chapter has focused attention on the contributions of Robert Montgomery's writing to the area of industrial organization, it must not be inferred that his accomplishments were limited to scholarship in just that field. The broad picture of his work shows wide-ranging concerns in social and political economy, steady involvement in practical policy-making, and long-lasting enthusiasm for teaching. In 1970 he wrote,

> During my extensive career in research, teaching, and operating in the general area of public utility regulation, my own basic interests have changed. The article that is being republished herewith represented for its day the best means I could devise for an acceptable—and workable—solution of our problems in that area.
>
> During the 40 years since that article was published in the *Quarterly* I have become convinced that the problem area discussed in the article is only one tiny segment of a vastly larger, more complex, more vital and more universal problem of Earth-Man (Montgomery 1970, p. 881).

During the 1920s and 1930s, while Montgomery had been focusing his attention on specific problems of competition, monopoly and regulation, he had also been developing a great deal of insight and some strong views regarding the social and historical context in which economic institutions evolve. The connection he saw between economic organization and democracy, implicit in his works on cotton cooperatives and more obvious in *The Brimstone Game*, were given specific attention in a series of articles in the 1930s in the *American Federationist*. In later years he turned his ironic wit to the production of parables that highlighted the central role of technology in determining institutions.

Perhaps it is simplest to say that Montgomery considered the "economic man" to be inseparable from the social man and the political man. He viewed economic motivations as bound up with other human drives and values, and economic organization as central to social and political rationality:

For a very long time man has worked and planned and fought for the things he has needed: food and clothing and shelter. We have wanted better homes, a little leisure, a chance to get ahead in the world; an opportunity to use our intelligence, our strength, our skill for our own betterment; an opportunity to govern ourselves; the right to make our own decisions in our own way; the chance to live in peace and dignity and mutual helpfulness with our neighbors. These are the foundation stones of the American system and of any other system of human society worthy of free men (Montgomery 1940, p. 91).

It is in this context that Montgomery saw economic problems—problems with competition or problems with monopoly—as not just inefficient but also undemocratic and socially destructive.

With this deep conviction that proper economic organization was essential to social health, Montgomery undertook important roles in the formation of pragmatic policy. He served for years as public defender of many cities in Texas, including Austin, in their rate proceedings involving Southwestern Bell" (Erickson n.d., p. 8). 'A million dollars worth of talent' against 'one little volunteer college professor', he once told a reporter. When that professor was Montgomery the odds were slightly in favor of the city of Austin" (Breit 1970, p. 863).

Robert Montgomery also served the nation. His concern for democratic institutions and outcomes motivated him to play policy advising roles in Washington, as the country first confronted the challenges of the Great Depression, then the economic issues of World War II.

Student of the world, scholar in industrial organization, civil servant at the local and national levels—but was Dr. Bob notable as a teacher? William Breit recalled:

When I first saw Montgomery in 1953, he was somewhat of a celebrity on campus. He affected a Stetson hat, cowboy boots, string tie and a tweed sport jacket that had a belt on the back. His lush head of greying hair and long bushy sideburns were unusual in those days of crew cuts, smugness and Senator McCarthy the First. And when he made a point loaded with what he took to be irony his blue eyes would light up beneath his wagging eyebrows and his face was all smiles. He was a flamboyant and colorful lecturer who understood the effectiveness of hyperbole in getting across an important point. His wit, intelligence and dramatic flair suggested that he would have made a great courtroom lawyer. Happily for the students at Texas he chose the classroom to display his forensic abilities. After hearing him the first time I didn't hit ground for two weeks (Breit 1970, pp. 862-863).

Perhaps Montgomery inherited his oratory skills from his preacher father; certainly he presented his ideas with conviction and sense of mission. His spellbinding style of teaching by storytelling—evident early in *The Brimstone Game* and late in his article "Like It Is: The Impact of Science on Culture"—surely dominated his classroom presentations and drew students to the issues he emphasized. Maurice Erickson reports that a new labor attaché in the Department of State said, after hearing Montgomery speak in 1944, "I learned more economics in one-half hour than I did at Harvard in four years" (Erickson n.d., p. 9).

But to return finally to Montgomery the industrial organizationist: his contributions in that area are important in part because they display many of the essential concerns that characterize Institutionalism and the Texas School; and they are important in part because they destroy the myth prevalent among many economists that the institutionalists at The University of Texas at Austin during the period 1930 to 1960 were "outside the mainstream." Just as Clarence Ayres provided valuable insights for development economists, Montgomery did the same in the area of industrial organization, or as it was known at UT until recently, the social control of industry. In many ways, the Texas School economists were outside the mainstream only in the sense that they served as forerunners; they made pioneering contributions that eventually became accepted within the mainstream of economics.

* * *

To my knowledge, Dr. Bob never came up with his ten-page version of "The Essential Montgomery." No one could do it but he, for the rest of us risk omitting what is most important and highlighting what is least. I hope I have not transgressed much.

ACKNOWLEDGMENTS

I am heavily indebted to Ronnie Phillips for his support in this project, to Maurice Erickson for his unpublished summary of Montgomery's work, to Harry Trebing for some early helpful criticism, and to many others who supplied details about Montgomery as scholar, teacher, and public servant.

NOTES

1. Story related by Roger Troub in personal correspondence with Ronnie Phillips, November 9, 1986.

2. For more on the "Texas School" see Ronnie J. Phillips, "Is There a Texas School of Economics," *Journal of Economic Issues 23* (September 1989): 863-872. Also see Ron Phillips, "Radical Institutionalism and the Texas School of Economics," in *Radical Institutionalism: Contemporary Voices*, edited by William M. Dugger, Westport, CT: Greenwood Press, 1989, pp. 21-37.

3. The literature generally traces these ideas to Joseph Bain, "A Note on Pricing in Monopoly and Oligopoly," *American Economic Review 39*: 448-464.

4. We may note, however, that a "ready-to-serve" charge manifests itself as a minimum bill, an approach frequently attacked by consumer advocates and liberal economists as inequitable and unduly restrictive of consumer choice (Harry Trebing, personal correspondence of 5 September 1989).

5. See, for example, Martin Glaeser, *Outlines of Public Utility Economics* (Macmillan 1927). Glaeser a was student of John R. Commons.

6. Harry Trebing, personal correspondence with the author, 5 September 1989.

7. Frederick Scherer, "The Development of the TD-X and TD-2 Microwave Radio Relay Systems in Bell Telephone Laboratories" (Weapons Acquisition Research Project, Harvard University, mimeo, October 1966). Cited by Harry Trebing, personal correspondence, 5 September 1989.

Chapter 5

Ruth Allen: Frontier Labor Economist

Alexandra Bernasek and Douglas Kinnear

I. BIOGRAPHICAL SKETCH OF RUTH ALLEN[1]

Born in Cameron, Texas in 1889, Ruth Alice Allen was a lifelong Texan. She received her B.A. in 1921 and her M.A. in 1923, both from the University of Texas, before going to the University of Chicago for her Ph.D. Even though she earned her doctorate from Chicago, she returned to Texas for a dissertation topic and the result was her first major work, *The Labor of Women in the Production of Cotton*, completed in 1933 under her advisor, H.A. Millis, and a committee that included Paul Douglas, Frank Knight, and Lloyd Mints. After receiving the Ph.D. she returned to UT, where she taught until her retirement in 1959.

Allen's tenure at Texas included a short stint as department chair (1942-43) and a longer term, encompassing most of the 1940s and 1950s, as the department's graduate advisor. Her devotion to education is evidenced by the fact that she spent six years of her retirement at Huston-Tillotson College, a predominantly black school in Texas, in order to preserve its accreditation. In 1968, at the age of 79, Allen began her final retirement, and in 1979 she died at the age of 90. Upon her death, the University of Texas faculty passed a memorial resolution noting that Allen "made her way to the professorship in times when this was close to impossible for a woman."[2] In the process, Ruth Allen undoubtedly helped break down some of the barriers to women who followed her into the profession. In addition to her contribution as a role model for women, she offered what was probably one of the first courses in the country that examined the economic position of women, entitled "The Economic Status of Women."

According to Forest Hill, one of Allen's students during her tenure at UT, she was a demanding professor who required from her students clear thinking and writing. When teaching in her areas of specialization, labor economics and economic history, she presented in-depth analyses of wide-ranging views, refusing to dogmatically adhere to any particular interpretation. An indication of her analytical disposition can be inferred from Hill's recollection that when teaching labor history, Allen's principle reference was *The History of Labor in the United States*, the landmark 1940 work by John R. Commons and his associates. Indeed, when looking back over Allen's works, her methodological tendencies seem to be similar to those of the institutionalist thinkers of her day, characterized by an aversion to abstract theorizing combined with a predisposition toward examining the ways that history and custom impact peoples' economic decision-making. Additionally, she shared the penchant for field work that was so common to labor economists, like Commons, of that era.

II. RUTH ALLEN'S RESEARCH

Her Methodology as a Labor Economist and Economic Historian

In the years between the two world wars, American labor economics was in a state of transition: while moving away from the earlier method of historical, empirical study of real-world labor problems, it shifted closer to becoming a subset of mainstream economic theory by applying the price-auction model to labor market processes, albeit often with heavy qualification. The earlier approach, which had been strongly influenced by the German historical school, emphasized the collecting of empirical information followed by historical and inductive analysis that was relatively devoid of abstract theorizing; a major part of this methodology involves close scrutiny of the institutions in the relevant market. Ruth Allen's work falls squarely in this tradition, as is demonstrated by a statement in the Introduction to her 1941 monograph *Chapters in the History of Organized Labor in Texas*: "It is upon frontiers, not geographical only, but economic, social and ideological, that the task of clarification must be done. There conflicting attitudes, situations, and institutional forms meet, rebound and merge into temporary operational patterns" (Allen 1941, p. 11). Thus, she does not favor taking institutions as given and static, as was the tendency for some later labor economists, but rather advocated study of the institutions themselves. She was not a theoretical institutionalist; rather, she examined the actual institutions of the markets she was studying, often focusing her analyses on subcultures of laborers, such as women in the production of cotton and lumber workers in east Texas.

This interpretation is confirmed by Forest Hill, who labels Allen an "eclectic institutionalist" on the basis of her interest in the role of socioeconomic institutions in shaping human behavior. But, as he also points out, she was not a theoretical institutionalist in the vein of her fellow UT faculty member Clarence Ayres or Thorstein Veblen; while they searched out the universal, instrumental values, Allen scrutinized actual institutions to find how they impacted peoples' everyday lives. Nowhere is this more evident than in her research into women involved in the production of cotton. Instead of attempting to fit all of their behavior into the cost-benefit calculus of mainstream economic theory, Allen was willing to allow for social institutions to influence peoples' behavior outside of the realm of so-called 'rational economic behavior'. Indeed, this book is a classic institutionalist analysis of the role of culture and tradition in allocating labor.[3]

Beyond this, Ruth Allen's work is strongly empirical and historical, fact-based in the extreme, and in her two major works, *The Labor of Women in the Production of Cotton* and *East Texas Lumber Workers*, she clearly shows her concern with real-world problems and finding solutions to them. It is of particular interest that these works both focus on the role of tradition and habit in creating a chronically impoverished group of workers. Her emphasis on real-world phenomena comes at a price, though, as Allen displays an aversion to abstract theorizing so extreme that the reader is sometimes left to piece together sections of analysis for herself. In the following discussions of Allen's works, we will attempt to bring her methodology and main themes into sharp relief.

The Labor of Women in the Production of Cotton

> Yet, strange to say, economists have almost universally ignored the strategic position occupied by women in any competitive struggle. And the failure to analyze clearly many of the difficult problems of modern industrial life is due to this hiatus in theoretical speculation and in actual observation. (Allen 1933, p. 250).

Allen is concerned in this work, her doctoral dissertation, with an investigation into "the life and work of women who live on the cotton farms of Texas" (Allen 1933, p. 11). The approach is socio-economic and methodologically fits in with the institutionalist approach to economic inquiry rather than the neoclassical. Allen considers the group of farm women that she studies significant for a number of reasons, the main one from her perspective being their relationship to the price of cotton and to the lives of the people living in farm families involved in the production of cotton. In her own words,

> The group of women just defined is significant from several viewpoints. First, it is intimately involved in the long-continued depression in the farming industry. The standard of living, the kind of work done, and all the phases of their social and economic life are tied inextricably to the price of cotton. Consequently, some knowledge

of the group may lead to a clearer light upon the manifold forces at work in determining the amount of cotton produced and the resulting price (Allen, 1933, p. 12).

Her two major areas of investigation are (1) the labor supply decision of the farm woman and (2) the implications of this for the production of cotton. In the first case she is interested in finding out what determines the kind of work women do: non-field work which includes work in the home, or field work in the production of cotton. She concludes that the type of work done by women is influenced more by tradition and custom than by economic costs and benefits. Understanding the economic and industrial meaning of this group of workers, she argues, is difficult because "it is so closely linked with the emotional and traditional basis of family life" (Allen 1933, p. 131). Later she reiterates her point:

Let it be repeated, the problem of the labor of women in the production of cotton, is woven into the warp and woof of the civilization of the southern cotton economy (Allen 1933, p. 146).

In the second case she finds that since the allocation of labor bears little relation to the cost of that labor, the price of cotton bears little relation to the true cost of producing it. She concludes that the unpaid labor of women in the production of cotton depresses the wages of farm workers and leads to overproduction of cotton, which keeps the price of cotton artificially low and perpetuates depressed farm incomes.

Allen places women at the center of the farm problem and at the center of its resolution. Before we discuss this, though, it will be instructive to describe her methodology and her conclusions. This book, like Allen's subsequent works, is characterized by a wealth of detailed information peppered with her insights. In the following summary we will focus on the main features of the analysis.

Allen seeks to answer a series of questions in this research. She does not always state the questions as explicitly as we state them here, but in many cases they are implied by the information that she sought to collect. She begins by analyzing the relationship between the home and social background of the women and the type of work they do. She then examines the determinants of a woman's position as either a field or non-field worker. For those women who work in the field she examines the determinants of whether they work for hire or for their families. And, finally, she tries to find out why some of the women provide unpaid labor in the field for their families. The answers to these questions reveal a system of production that is detrimental to the women and in turn to their families.

The method of inquiry Allen used for this research was a survey of women in farm households in Texas. She designed the survey instrument herself: a questionnaire directed to the women of the farm households; and she conducted the majority of the interviews personally. The interviewing was done over a period of 15 months, from November 1928 to January 1930. She reports that the greatest difficulty she encountered was "the lack of knowledge on the part of the women themselves" (Allen 1933, p. 31), especially with respect to the exact amount of work done in any part of their lives. Since Allen conducted most of the interviews herself, her empirical data is supplemented by a wealth of personal observations on and reactions to the women she met and their living and working conditions.

A common characteristic of her work is a concern with the effects of racial and ethnic differences among workers. In this study she begins with a broad classification of women into three groups according to race/ethnicity: American (white), Negro (black), and Mexican (Hispanic origin).[4] She separately investigates the women in each group on the basis of their home and social background and on the basis of the work they perform. She wants to explain the type of work they do, non-field work or field work, and also to analyze the conditions of the work. Toward this end, she initially subdivides the women into two groups: those engaged in field work and those who perform non-field work. The field workers are further subdivided according to whether they work for hire only, for the family and for hire, or for the family only. As an indicator of the economic status of the farm family, and thus as an indicator of the effect of economic necessity on the type of work women do, she makes use of a classification of households according to their land tenure status as owners, tenants, or landless laborers.

Allen's classification of women according to the type of work they perform is significant because of the fact that it differs from the definition in the census. Allen classifies women as "field workers" if they report having worked in the field for two weeks or more in the past year. Based on her definition approximately fifty percent of the women surveyed fall into the two categories of field worker and non-field worker. According to the census definition the proportions would be ten percent field workers and ninety percent non-field workers. A concern of feminists is that official estimates like those of the census grossly underestimate the productive contributions of women. In this respect Allen shows a willingness to utilize a more realistic measure of women's participation in farm production.

Intertwined with her description and analysis of the data are Allen's own observations and interpretations and her attempts to link these to the broader social context. There are numerous examples of this. One is a discussion of the effects of the automobile on the farm family and on society generally. She first writes:

> Under the old carless regime, the masculine members of the household got out their horses, saddled them, and rode away unquestioned. There was no room to take the wife, daughter, or sister; and there was no room for argument or protest. There is room in the car, and when the car goes the wife and daughters get in, and again there is little room for protest. The man has lost his liberty. No longer is "going to town" the open sesame to a few hours of absolutely uncensored life. A greatly privileged class is passing, and it may be by such seemingly unimportant changes as this that civilizations are undermined and social systems fall (Allen 1933, pp. 40-41).

One cannot help but wonder after reading this whether Allen was writing it "tongue in cheek" or whether her delivery was just so dry as to make it appear so. If it is the former, then it is still probably true that there was an element of seriousness in what she wrote. She goes on to discuss the effects of the automobile on farm women and on the farm household:

> The effect of this change has an effect upon the farm home which it is difficult to estimate, for the woman was the stable element in farm life. She was always there, carrying on her duties and keeping things together, doing odd jobs that could not be neglected. That stable element is disappearing..... The woman has gained a wider horizon, but is it wide enough to replace in mental and spiritual values the physical production of which she was formerly the center? Has she not gained a discontent that can hardly be classed as divine and an unwillingness to perform the old tasks with neither the willingness, the knowledge, nor the opportunity to perform the new ones? In this she is not peculiar. In common with thousands of other women she is demanding liberty without accepting the fact that real freedom is functional freedom. The loss to the farm home may be almost fatal, but it is not necessarily so to society (Allen 1933, p. 41).

Another example of this can be found in her discussion of the transition taking place in the post World War II period, with the majority of the population moving from a rural to an urban way of life. Connected with the growth of the urban population Allen predicts that factories will draw on the labor supply of women and girls and that knowledge of their existing standards of work and living would provide some understanding of

> ....the place the women will fill as workers and as bargainers in the new system and will enable the social group to guard itself and them from paying a greater price than is necessary for the transition (Allen 1933, p. 14).

This theme of social and economic change, particularly as it applies to young women and their willingness to remain on the farm, is one that fits into the center of Allen's assessment of the prospects for the future of the farm family. We will explore this further, but before doing so we will summarize the process through which she develops her assessment.

Beginning with an investigation of the American Woman, Allen asks the question "Why does the American Woman become a field-worker?" (In her sample approximately one half of the women are classified as field workers and one half as non-field workers.) What she finds in answer to that is that there are several factors that can account for the type of work a woman will do. There is a distinct economic factor involved, as evidenced by the proportions of the two groups among the different tenure classes. The smallest proportion of field workers was found in the group of owners and the largest proportion was found in the class of landless laborers. Allen writes: "It will be noted that as the women sink in the scale economically, as indicated by their tenure class, a larger percentage become field workers" (Allen 1933, p. 78).

Economic need, then, is one reason for women to work in the field. Another factor appears to be the nature of the woman's tie to the family. More than three fourths of the unmarried women did field work, while only two fifths of the married women and half of the widows surveyed worked in the field. "It appears, then, and further analysis will strengthen the conclusion, that the married woman living with her husband is less likely than the woman of any other group of women to do field work" (Allen, 1933, p. 79).

For the American woman another factor appears to be the number of people for whom housework needs to be done. The number of children in the family and the number of other females in the family are both found to have some effect on whether the woman is released from working in the field (Allen 1933, p. 83).

Allen also relates the number of children in the family to the mother's economic status, the best measure of which she says is the tenure status of the family. In the process she attempts to dispel one of the myths surrounding the "economic value of children." She finds that there is a tendency to smaller families among the tenants but that at either of the other two ends, the owners and the landless laborers tended to have relatively large families. Among the laboring families Allen raises the possibility that the large families can be explained by the hypothesis that children are economic assets to their parents. She questions that as a valid explanation by asking whether the phrase "children are an economic asset" is not rather "an empty phrase which has gained a position of respect because of much mouthing by economists and non-economists" (Allen 1933, p. 70). She gets to the heart of the matter, in terms of children as assets to their mothers, with the following analysis,

> If children be an economic asset, why does a woman who has borne fifteen and lived all her life in the farm find herself at eighty three without house or land, living in a hovel, her title to which depends on an old man with whom she has formed an economic partnership? Somehow her assets have never materialized to the extent that they could give her a living. If children be economic assets, why is it that of the twenty three women in the entire group of field workers who report families of eight or more, twenty one are in the families of non-land owners? ...... But it seems the more assets a family has the deeper the family sinks into the economic slough (Allen 1933, p. 70).

When considering the work performed by non-field workers, Allen is concerned with somehow valuing that work and comparing it to the work performed by field workers. The tasks of non-field workers are mainly housekeeping and the auxiliary duties associated with life on the farm. On the definition of such work she writes: "The methods and implements of work are comparatively crude. The four tasks of the housewife are cooking, sewing, house cleaning, and washing and ironing" (Allen 1933, p. 42). As Allen points out, these tasks are made difficult by the crude equipment owned by the families. The women mainly relied upon wood (which had to be collected and chopped) as fuel for cooking and heat, kerosene lamps (which had to be constantly filled) for light, hauled water for laundry and bathing, and their own hands for sewing.

Allen also includes a description of what she later refers to as the "extra-routine housework" on the farm:

> Housework on the farm includes many processes which are not now considered a part of the operation of the town home. Such items which immediately come to mind are raising chickens, caring for a garden and caring for milk. Also much more sewing and more preserving of foods, processes which have passed from the town home, are done in the farm home (Allen 1933, p. 84).

Allen on non-field workers and home production:

Labor costs based on tradition and sentimentality may be at the very root of the problem. So long as there is no clear relation between labor costs and production, there can be no definite relation between labor cost and price (Allen 1933, p. 95).

Allen is concerned with the value of home production. She argues that reductions in household expenditures are equivalent to increases in household income. She wants to determine the value of the time that women spend in home production, reducing the families' expenditures, compared with the value of the time that women spend in the field increasing family income. Allen asks the question, "Field work is not itself undesirable for women on the farm, but is it more economical for the farm and the family that the woman should do that rather than other work?" (Allen 1933, pp. 86-87).

Neoclassical economic theory would predict that if women were engaging in field work rather than work in the home it must be because that represents an efficient allocation of their labor. Allen's findings challenge that neoclassical prediction. Because there is no formal accounting of women's labor time, both in the field and in the home, Allen finds it difficult to determine what the "rational economic allocation" of labor should be. By taking a socio-economic perspective she is able to suggest non-economic reasons for the allocation of women's labor.

Characteristic of Allen's work is a rigorous attention to detail, as exemplified by her calculation of the value of goods produced in the home by women who do no field work. She averaged the quantity of canned and preserved goods produced at home by a sub sample of the non-field working women, and then priced the goods at a large chain store. Other home produced goods that she considered included soap, vegetables, milk, chickens, turkeys, eggs, quilts, and clothing. On the basis of her calculations she found that the average annual money value of home production for these women was $442.69. For those who earned a cash income from the sale of these goods the amount was $603.95. She then compared this to the average annual value of the labor of women who work in the field, which she finds is $61.30. Her reaction to this is to comment:

In view of this one is led to wonder just what is meant by the common statement that 'cotton is the only ready money crop'. Because of this credo women must work in the production of cotton, yet it seems that women who do not help raise cotton bring in more money than women who do (Allen 1933, p. 92).

The comparison of the figures is so striking that one wonders how this state of affairs could persist. Allen's explanation is "bookkeeping." She essentially argues that finding economical alternatives to the production of cotton would require intelligent bookkeeping by the farm families, an outcome which she finds unlikely: "In the face of such ignorance and indifference to the financial organization of the farm, cotton is easily handled and calculated. As long as this is true, there will be a necessity for women to work in the production of cotton as the ready money crop" (p. 93). Thus the family farm accounting system, such as it is, fails to provide a rational measure of the value of women's labor.

At this point the reader is left with the distinct impression that women should leave the fields and concentrate on home production. But Allen does not let us off the hook that easily. First, she argues that if all women were to concentrate on home production, the market for such goods would be flooded, making such production economically infeasible. Second, she argues that the income from home production cannot be treated as a net addition to total income because none of the input costs have been netted out. As she writes, "It is possible and it may be probable that the cost if charged against the products would reduce the income by a considerable amount or even cause it to disappear" (Allen 1933, p. 94).

The reader is then forced to ask why women would engage in such production if it was not economical? Allen has some explanations for this, too. Again, they reflect her willingness to go beyond the economic, when it seems incapable of explanation, and to consider possible socio-cultural explanations.

It is also probable, and in many cases certain that the raising of chickens and the caring for milk is a personal assertion by the woman of her economic worth. Home production furnishes a method of getting money of her own for which she has neither to ask or give an account. It is possible that it is also the husband's method of indulging his wife's desire for work and it may really cost more than it brings in (Allen 1933, p. 94).

Work as a "personal assertion" and a "desire for work" are words clearly at odds with the mainstream view, in which people dislike work and only perform it if the utility from the financial reward exceeds the disutility of the work itself. Far from viewing work as painful, Allen understands that some of these women, who are economically able, actually engage in productive activity because they *like* it. Allen's view of work is thus similar to that of many institutionalists, including Thorstein Veblen, who see in humans an innate drive toward productive effort. Nonetheless, a precondition for such work is that the family can afford to have one of its members engaged in work that doesn't earn enough to cover its cost. Thus, one would expect that it is predominantly among the wealthier families that women would be engaged in home production. The majority of the non-field working women and the majority of those engaged in home production were found by Allen in the families of land owners. She adds:

Women in the higher economic classes in the country turn to such production as the town woman turns to tea shops and handiwork.... Among the farm women, as in the other groups, it is the woman in the more fortunate classes financially to whom these sources of personal income are open. For the less fortunate, there must be hired labor, and even then it may yield no personal income (Allen 1933, pp. 94-95).

Here we get a hint of what is to come. So far it has been established that one of the principal factors affecting a woman's work status is economic necessity, but that from the farm families' perspective, field work may not represent the most efficient allocation of labor.

Allen on women's field work in the production of cotton:

Turning to a more detailed investigation of the field workers, Allen asks the question, "Why does the American farm woman work in the field?" The reason that women work for hire in addition to working in the field for their families is economic necessity: the largest proportion of field workers were found in the families of the tenant class. Among those who work for hire, though, she also finds a distinction on the basis of marital status. Unmarried women are more likely to work because it provides them with an "outlet" (Allen 1933, p. 126), a way of earning a personal income, independent of the economic need of the family. Allen supports this with the evidence that the majority of the unmarried girls who worked for hire were from the families of owners. Married women on the other hand worked for hire out of economic necessity.

The group of women Allen is most interested in, and the group that she sees as central to the miserable position of women and to the farm problem, is the group of women who provide unpaid labor in the field to their families. One of the crucial things that she does is to actually establish that this labor is in fact unpaid, that it is not, contrary to what many have argued, labor provided to "earn" the woman's room and board. By recognizing and measuring the household work that women perform, Allen is able to establish that it is this work that "earns" the woman her room and board and to which her field work is an unpaid addition.

> The greatest possible fallacy in the computation of the amount of cotton put on the market with no commensurate return for the labor performed by women of the producers' families is the assumption, previously mentioned, that the women do get their living (Allen 1933, p. 154).

In a distinctly feminist tone she goes on to say,

> It is useless to insist that the services of wife, mother and daughter in the home are not to be evaluated in terms of money. Here it is not a question of estimating the value of immaterial and sentimental services but of determining the effect upon a distinctly material good, the cotton crop of the State (Allen 1933, p. 154).

Looking at different types of households in terms of the number of women in the household and thus the number of women contributing to household work, Allen finds the following:

> The market value of these services alone would balance any account for living expenses (Allen 1933, p. 155).

> Any labor given by these women to the production of cotton is unquestionably a gift.... The women pay for more than they "eat and the clothes they wear" by household services rendered; and in addition they make it possible to put on the market thousands of pounds of cotton to which no possible method of rationalization can give a labor cost (Allen 1933, p. 157).

In this situation, and in Allen's analysis, the neoclassical theory of wage determination is nowhere to be found. The value of the marginal product of the labor of these women is clearly not zero, and yet they are paid no wage. Here again we see the institutionalist character of Allen's work. By looking at the social relations of production she is able to find an explanation beyond the neoclassical to explain the allocation of women's labor to field work. Custom and tradition, not the marginal productivity of women, explains the supply of their unpaid labor to the production of cotton for their families.

Allen meticulously calculates the value of the unpaid labor that women give to the cotton crop (Allen 1933, pp. 151-153). From reports on the amount of cotton picked, Allen calculates an average of approximately 200 pounds per day. She estimates a conservative wage rate for pickers of $1.15 per hundred pounds. She obtains information on the average prices of cotton from the Department of Agriculture for the years 1920-1928 inclusive and calculates a mean price of 18.2 cents. The total money wages that the women would receive at the going rate was found to be $24,965.15, which turned out to be $130 per person. At the average price of cotton 1.4 bales would be required to pay that average wage. If each woman gives the equivalent of 1.4 bales of cotton to the market, and generalizing the proportions of women in this group to the rest of the state, then we would have 137,379 women providing unpaid labor; 164,855 bales of cotton would be required to pay their wages.[5] Given that the yearly cotton crop of Texas was estimated at 5,150,000 bales of cotton, these women, by withholding their labor, could reduce production by one thirtieth.

"How then shall we estimate the cost of production of cotton?" (Allen 1933, p. 169). The production of cotton, Allen discovers, bears no relation to the cost of the labor that produces it. The only way this situation can persist, she argues, is with a farming system organized on the principle of a household industry and "group labor." There is no such thing as individual labor within this system. But she predicts that the system will not continue for long:

> But the twentieth century is a century of machines, of individual incomes, of individual production, of the almost completed passing of production from the home to the factory. It avails not to sing of the beauties of family life, of groups living and working together. Such beauties, if there are any, exist at a great cost to those who cannot meet the requirements of that system, and who are helpless before the pressure of a factory age (Allen 1933, pp. 169-170).

Allen on the role of racial/ethnic differences in women's labor in the production of cotton:

> One is somewhat forced to the conclusion that between the three groups described in this paper, a relentless if silent struggle for survival is taking place (Allen 1933, p. 250).

A sub-plot to this investigation is the dynamic that Allen uncovers between the three racial/ethnic groups. She perceives a competitive struggle for survival taking place between the American, Negro, and Mexican farm families. To understand her conclusions it is useful to point out some of the main differences among the American, Negro and Mexican farm women.

Allen finds that the average size and composition of households differed among the three groups. Many more American women lived in households with only one female. Earlier in the book she writes,

5. The burden of the mother who has no one to help her with the housework and yet works in the field is very heavy, more so probably than the double burden of the industrial worker.
6. Families having two or more adult women are in a very favorable situation with regard to labor costs in the production of cotton (Allen 1933, p. 172).

She also finds a higher proportion of field workers among the Negro women (86.5%) and the Mexican women (56.5%) than among the American women (45%). This may be explained partly by the larger proportion of both Negroes and Mexicans in the lower economic classes of the tenants and laborers. It may also be related to the size and composition of the households. The average household size was smallest for the Americans (5.5 persons) and largest for the Mexicans (8.4 persons) with the Negroes in the middle (7.1 persons). In both the Negro and Mexican households Allen found that it was not uncommon to have extended family members present. That was much less common among the households of the American women. "There can be little question that the comparatively small amount of field work done by the American women is connected with the more complete synonymy of the family with the household among the Americans" (Allen 1933, p. 241).

Probably the most significant factor for Allen in distinguishing the three groups is the absence of young girls among the American families. She argues that American girls leave home more readily than girls from either of the other two groups. Allen sees this as having a significant effect on the competitive struggle occurring among the three groups. She writes, "The failure of the American young person to stay on the farm and help raise the crop is unquestionably one reason for the failure of the American to hold his place in competition for the position as pillars of the cotton economy" (Allen 1933, p. 242).

Given her perception of the decline of the American farm family, Allen concentrates on the competition between the Negro and the Mexican. If sheer numbers are to be the determining factor in the struggle then she sees the Mexican farm family winning over the Negro. In this respect the Mexican woman is more willing to bear large numbers of children than the Negro woman. The proportion of Negro women with no children was much larger than the proportions of either American or Mexican women.

When she compares the standard of living of the Mexican and Negro families she finds another area in which the Mexican family has an edge over the Negro:

> It would appear, then, that the Mexican woman has a willingness to accept a lower standard of living than either the Negro or the American white. And, furthermore, her standard is so much lower than that even of the Negro that it will be an important factor in any economic competition (Allen 1933, p. 246).

The only aspect of this competitive struggle in which Allen sees the Negro having the edge over the Mexican is in the efficiency with which field work is performed. The outcome of the struggle is thus uncertain. On two of the three counts the Mexican has the advantage but that may not be enough to guarantee victory.

Allen on the solution to the problem of women in the production of cotton:

> It would appear from the facts here presented that the attitude of each of the groups to its women and of the women themselves toward the part they play in the social economy, is a large factor in survival and in the type of survival (Allen 1933, p. 250).

Allen places women at the center of the farm problem and at the center of its solution. The solution, according to Allen, is for women to be paid for all of their labor, whether it be in the household or in the field. She writes,

> It is along the lines of a greater increase in hired labor that the remedy for the evils pointed out as characterizing the position of the farm woman seems to lie. The woman in the farm family must be given work which will add to the family income, and she may secure this income only as a worker for wages (Allen 1933, p. 249).

Allen is concerned lest all women flee to the towns seeking an income. She does not think the answer lies in a mass exodus of women from farms, however, as this will only result in a transfer of their miserable living standards from the farm to the town. Rather, she recommends that some should stay in farm work when it is rational:

> Many should remain in farm work, but not in a situation in which they are drained physically, mentally and spiritually in order to fill an already overstocked market in which the cost of production has little or no relation to the cost of living of human beings (Allen 1933, p. 249).

She reiterates the economic irrationality of the extant system of cotton production and argues that applying a wage system to all workers will actually increase farm income. In her own words, "If farm production were organized so that all labor would be wage labor, the work of the woman would make an addition to family income instead of decreasing it by the very act of performing that labor" (Allen 1933, p. 249).

Here she seems to be arguing that the unpaid labor of women leads to overproduction of cotton, and this in turn depresses the price of cotton and farm income. If women are paid for their labor, farm wages will increase, the production of cotton will decrease, the price of cotton will rise and presumably income will increase, assuming, as we believe she does, that the demand for cotton is price inelastic.

Given the socio-economics of cotton production in Texas, Allen recognizes two possible trends for the future. One is no reduction in the numbers of farmers and the consequent reduction in their living standards. The other involves fewer farmers, but a higher standard of living. Allen feels that women control the future, as they determine the number of laborers and hence the standard of living: "Whichever method of survival, then, is chosen, the women hold both kings and aces" (Allen 1933, p. 250).

She draws broader implications in the conclusion to her paper. She is concerned that, should the first scenario prevail, the resulting standard of living will threaten not only rural life but the urban sector as well. She argues that a large supply of cheap, unskilled labor will drive down its own wage rates and, through a reduction of purchasing power, those of skilled and professional workers as well. Further, she urges "...that the standard of living here described, however bearable in rural life shall not be exploited to fill our cities with overcrowded slums" (Allen 1933, p. 265). The crux of her interpretation of the farm problem is restated succinctly at the end of the paper:

> Here is, also, a group of laborers, working in one of the major industries of the country and forming a considerable part of the entire labor force of that industry, whose return is set entirely without the wage market. Further the supply of labor in the industry is settled without relation to a market demand for laborers. It is instead determined largely by timeworn standards and ideas as to the function of the family and the function of the women of the group (Allen 1933, p. 265).

And the solution that she proposes follows closely.

> It seems probable that the only hope lies in an organization of the industry which will bring with it the forces of market control as to wages, as to labor supply, and as to price...... All field labor on cotton farms should become wage labor so that those performing the labor may be paid an amount equal to at least that of unskilled labor in other industries of the section (Allen 1933, pp. 265-266).

How will this change women's work? Allen argues that the disappearance of home production would not be a loss, since its value would be surpassed by women's earnings in the field. She likewise sees no problem with some field workers moving into other occupations, as long as they are paid wages for their time. "Will not such a change, among other things, bring a partial justice to still another group of people who are victims of the tradition of the family as a producing unit and of the fiction of the single wage earner family" (Allen 1933, p. 266).

We can credit Allen with being an early feminist economist. Her recognition of the family as a determinant of women's economic status foreshadows a central theme of contemporary feminist economics. Allen discovered the interaction of family relations with production by the family and made it the foundation of her analysis. This interaction, she determined, produces an inferior outcome for women and a system of production that is not economically rational. Like contemporary feminist economists, Allen also reveals the myth inherent in the common view of the husband as the only "worker." It is a widely held belief among contemporary feminist economists that if women were paid a wage for the work that they perform, that work would not continue to be invisible; Ruth Allen realized this in 1933.

Chapters in the History of Organized Labor in Texas

Chapters in the History of Organized Labor in Texas is merely a collection of information, amassed from court records, historical newspaper articles, union archives, library archives, census records, and personal remembrances, pertaining to the labor history of Texas. Allen apparently intended this as a record, a collection of data to be used for other research projects, and not an end in itself ("That we may face and judge the problems of the future, it is desirable now that we should investigate the components which make them up. This volume is an unimportant item in that investigation" (Allen 1941, p. 14)). The specific topics covered include a "cowboy strike" that occurred in 1883, a boycott of granite cutters against the construction of the Texas state capitol in the late 1880s, a "Sketch History of the Texas State Federation of Labor," and descriptions of the activities of the United Mine Workers in Texas and "The Negro in the State Federation of Labor." Allen presents a wealth of information on these topics, but does not really draw any general conclusions. Her rather straightforward presentation of the facts does, though, occasionally reveal a strong empathy for the common working people and those who were trying to organize the workers of various industries.

The Great Southwest Strike

In the 1942 monograph *The Great Southwest Strike*, Allen again mainly relays facts for the historical record; she also further displays her affinity for those who were promoting labor organizations in Texas in the late 1800s. Her prose often reads as if it came from the union literature of the time: "The industrialized society which emerged from the war between the states brought its inevitable concomitant, an industrial wage earning group, and the wage worker caught between the machine system with its pitilessly equalitarian force and the corporation with its crystallizing autocracy saw no clear picture of his place and status" (Allen 1942, p. 15). Allen neatly summarized the business dealings of Jay Gould, a major player in the strike, with more eloquence but, one thinks, probably no less contempt than would have been used by one of his striking employees in 1886: "Among all the fraternity of the 1880's skilled in the modes of stock manipulation; of transferring property between themselves, from the government, and from the people, Gould had acquired a malevolent transcendency" (Allen 1942, pp. 12-13). Gould, who had by 1886 bought and subsequently plundered several railroads so severely that they ended up in receivership, had less interest in shipping than he had in monopoly power over shipping rates in the southwest. This he largely achieved, and Allen notes that by 1882 his vast rail holdings made him the largest employer of labor in the southwest.

With Jay Gould painted as the villain, the role of hero in this story falls to Martin Irons. Irons was a roving machinist and unionist who had, by 1886, found himself in the employ of Gould's Missouri Pacific Railroad and chairman of the executive committee of District Assembly No. 101 of The Noble and United Order of the Knights of Labor. Allen painstakingly recounts all of the specific grievances and animosities that gave rise to a strike in March of 1886 by the Knights of Labor against Gould's line, but, as was probably clear to Irons at the time and is even more evident in retrospect, a broader issue was that the Knights were seeking recognition from Gould—recognition of their perceived right to represent their members in grievance proceedings. With meticulous attention to detail, Allen relates the events of the strike, including the ensuing violence and mass arrests that were so common to labor-management conflicts of the time. The national organization of the Knights was opposed to strikes, and District Assembly No. 101 was too young to have amassed a substantial strike fund, and as a result, the uprising eventually fell apart, and the railroad took back Knights only if they would affirm that they had nothing to do with the strike and would furthermore resign their membership in the organization.

The Great Southwest Strike of 1886 had been so damaging and violent, and created such grave fears for many in the nation, that President Grover Cleveland called for a congressional committee to investigate the discord. According to Allen's investigation, Martin Irons became the scapegoat, the embodiment of all that was despised and feared in organized labor; according to Allen's inquiry, this vilification was unjust, as Irons unfailingly followed the will of his men, never imposing his desires upon them. Nonetheless, the slander stuck to Martin Irons for the rest of his life, and he was effectively blacklisted from practicing his craft and was harassed virtually everywhere he tried to settle.

What insights does Allen draw from this significant episode in the labor history of the southwest? Without trying to veil her support for organized labor, she wrote:

> The failure of the strike threw the labor movement in the Southwest back upon itself, and the Southwest learned its lesson well. Not since the mid-eighties has there been a labor movement in the area and through the years with no forceful labor cooperation it has developed low wage scales, poor standards of living, a crass and naive emphasis upon the rights of property. When the contention is made that the Southwest does not want a labor movement, it does not fit the environment, the obvious answer is, 'There was once a labor movement in the Southwest, virile, courageous and hopeful. Had it not been completely broken it might have helped the section to a fuller development of economic life.' And not only the Southwest but the Nation (Allen 1942, p. 156).

The failure, she asserts, arose from the workers themselves: "The reason lies primarily in the characteristics of the workers themselves, in their lack of an ideological core, of a concept of the function of an organized labor movement in the mutually interdependent operation of economic life" (Allen 1942, p. 156). The strikers, Martin Irons included, were a distinctly American group, "authentic spokesmen for the dreams and ambitions of Americans." (Allen 1942, p. 157). In an inarticulate voice, they were expressing the attitudes, the hostilities, of all American laborers about the rise of monopoly capital in the United States. Allen is clearly on the populist side in this war between labor and profit-hungry businessmen, as evidenced by the last few lines of this manuscript:

> The corporation and those upon whose shoulders rest the mephisto-phelian robes of the financiers of the eighties still hold the citadels of power. The corporate machine system, the Southwest still wishes to escape. It refuses to take and tame it to a basis for material living upon which may be built good housing, good health, good schools, good food, good recreation. This cannot be done without taking into full partnership the ideological descendants of the Southwestern Strikers. But dread of facing the issue which they posited persists and mastery not travel with fear (Allen 1942, p. 158).

In this she is in accord with a traditional institutionalist theme: an affinity for productive effort along with a disdain for those who seek control of business merely for purposes of profit.

East Texas Lumber Workers

Although ostensibly an inquiry into the nature and causes of the deep and persistent poverty of the era in northeast Texas, an area with an economy driven by the lumber industry, the book is more aptly described by its subtitle: "An Economic and Social Picture, 1870-1950." In this work, Allen again displays her talent for amassing copious quantities of information. The problem, as in some of her other works, is a seeming unwillingness to marshal the data into a coherent picture that supports germane conclusions. When Allen does proffer an explanation for the region's poverty, it appears in the last chapter and, especially in light of the volume of facts that have preceded it, it receives scant support.

Allen does thoroughly illuminate the economic conditions of the lumber country of northeast Texas. She presents much demographic information on the region, fully supporting the Joint Committee of Congress which studied the 1950 *Economic Report of the President* and labeled the area as one of "deep poverty." The area, which she delineates as "roughly 32 counties lying north of Houston and east of Dallas" (Allen 1961, p. 5), is notable not for the absolute number of people living in poverty, she argues, but for the high proportion of residents living in deprivation. In these terms, the region is "undoubtedly one of comparative poverty in relation to the state, and since per-capita income of the state is below that of the United States, the poverty of this region in relation to the nation is notable" (Allen, 1961, p. 5). The area is comprised primarily of towns and small cities, and the economic life of the region is dominated by the lumber industry, with the highest proportion of jobs provided by logging and the manufacturing of lumber products. The population, as Allen explains, is poorly educated, has low mobility (as measured by the percentage of people who had lived in the same house for more than a year), and is predominately native Texan, with relatively few first-generation immigrants in the area.

Allen's methodology, her framework for making sense of the region, is eclectic and fundamentally institutionalist:

> A survey of the background of these people leads perforce to their lives as workers and, since their working environment has been largely conditioned by the forests in which they have lived and by the processing of its products, that environment, its history, and present-day achievements are of major interest (Allen 1961, p. 14).

Individuals, in their roles as workers, do not passively respond to costs and benefits; rather, the physical, social, and economic environment conditions their behavior. Of particular importance in the case of the east Texas lumber workers, Allen felt, is their isolation, both physical and intellectual. As pointed out, the vast majority of the workers in the lumber industries were native born Americans, and their educational attainment was, as a group, relatively low. This isolation and ignorance plays an important role in causing poverty in the region; after making a few references in the heart of the book to the immobility of the people in this region, in the final chapter she cites this characteristic as the cause of their poverty:

> Elaborate theoretical foundations are scarcely necessary to support the conclusion that incomes are low because there is generally, considering the wages offered, a more-than-sufficient supply of labor....It seems clear that low wages are accepted by laborers because they are immobile. The causes of this immobility are generally to be found in ignorance of economic possibilities-which are tied to illiteracy and fear of the unknown. A recent study of occupational mobility finds restrictions upon mobility inherent in unequal educational and vocational training opportunities and limited occupational ambitions (Allen 1961, pp. 193-194).

Thus, Allen does not accept the neoclassical presumption that mobility will lead to uniform wage rates for similar types of labor:

> When even the pressure of a low standard of living cannot impel laborers to move from one area to another even though there is no legal restriction against their migration (as might occur during wartimes), it means they are governed by barriers which prevent them from developing their economic capacities to the fullest... Their chain of cultural character- istics, developed through social situations similar to, but not synonymous with, those in the industrial life of a community, has been so strongly forged that it withstands the assault of economic pressure (Allen 1961, p. 196).

Of course, modern neoclassical theorists would simply argue that these workers were accepting a negative compensating wage differential because they preferred to live in northeastern Texas; or perhaps they would argue that these Texans had insufficient information on labor market possibilities, and with more complete knowledge they might have moved to the higher-wage areas, thus creating equalization of wage rates across the nation. Allen's argument that ignorance is a contributing factor to immobility is compatible with the second argument. But, we can't ignore the other half of her explanation: that "fear of the unknown" and a "chain of cultural characteristics" have bonded the population to a particular area. Neoclassicals, attempting to fit these facts into their model, would contend that the fear and the cultural bonds felt by the lumber workers are operationalized through compensating wage differentials, but this would obscure the reality of the situation. Allen's methodological bent does not allow her to force all decisions into dollar values; rather, she seems willing to allow workers' labor market decisions to be influenced by intangible criteria— and, unlike many younger labor economists trained after her, she makes no attempt to fit these criteria into the price-auction model. Yes, we must acknowledge that, substantively, her argument can be fit into the neoclassical model; but Allen's intended interpretation appears to be to the contrary. In this, *East Texas Lumber Workers* is consistent with Ruth Allen's other works.

Handbook of Texas

Allen also has ten entries in the *Handbook of Texas*, published in 1952, which reflect her interest in labor issues of Texas specifically and of the Southwest generally. Many of the entries are directly related to her research into organized labor in Texas. In particular, the entries "Martin Irons" and "Southwest Strike" come from the information in her monograph, *The Great Southwest Strike*. The entries, "Capitol Boycott", "Labor Organization in Texas", "The Cowboy Strike", and "Union Regulation in Texas" are all references from her monograph *Chapters in the History of Organized Labor in Texas*.

Additionally, she has an entry on "James W. Truitt", who was influential in setting up the Railroad Commission and who in 1877 along with John M. Bowman established a paper called *The Laborer's Champion*. Another entry discusses the history of "Child Labor Legislation in Texas." She also documents the history of the "Southwest Social Science Association" and its associated publication, the "Southwest Social Science Quarterly."

III. RUTH ALLEN'S CONTRIBUTION

Although *The Labor of Women in the Production of Cotton* was Ruth Allen's dissertation and first major work, it is nonetheless remarkably mature. In it we see themes that are strongly evident in her other major work, *East Texas Lumber Workers*, and that are also sometimes present to a lesser degree in her archival works. These include a focus on regional labor problems; the examination of a particular group of workers, often in terms of their socio-economic subculture, and how they fit into an institutional complex; and the ways that tradition and habit determine the allocation of labor. In both the *Labor of Women* and *Lumber Workers*, Allen preferred to collect large amounts of data from fieldwork and archival records, and then engage in highly inductive, fact-based analyses to reach her conclusions.

The only major element of her dissertation that does not appear in her study of lumber workers is gender. Whereas *The Labor of Women in the Production of Cotton* places much importance on the particular socio-economic position of farm women and how it induces them to supply labor, her later studies are devoid of any gender-specific analyses. Ironically, though, this work, and in particular its focus on gender roles in the allocation of labor, remains her most influential. A look at the Social Science Citation index over the last twenty years reveals twelve citations of Allen's work, with the most recent ones referencing *The Labor of Women in the Production of Cotton*.[6] As feminist scholarship has expanded it is not surprising that Allen's pioneering work on women would be rediscovered.

Joan M. Jensen in her article "Cloth, Butter, and Boarders: Women's Household Production for the Market" in the *Review of Radical Political Economics*, references the value of home production of the farm women in Allen's survey. Jensen argues in her article that women's household production, particularly the making of cloth and butter, was a crucial economic factor in rural families. She argues that with the disappearance of this type of production, women moved into the capitalist mode of production, away from household income and toward wage income.

Jensen uses Allen's estimates of the value of home production and her conclusion that it often exceeds the value of women's field production to support her own argument regarding the economic contribution that such production made to farm families. Interestingly, though, she does not mention what Allen goes on to state later in the book about home production: that even though it may not be economical in dollars and cents, it may nonetheless persist in families that can "afford" to let women spend time in such production, and furthermore that there would be no loss to the farm family if such home production were to disappear with the advent of a wage system for all farm labor. Allen is difficult to follow on the topic of home production and some of her statements seem to be contradictory. The contradictions, though, actually result from the system of allocating women's labor, which Allen argues was based on tradition and sentimentality within the family rather than rational economic accounting. In that case it becomes difficult, as Allen discovers, to determine the "true" value of home production compared to the "true" value of other productive activities for women.

Susan A. Mann in her article "Slavery, Sharecropping, and Sexual Inequality," also references the work of Allen on women in cotton production. She draws on Allen's observation, "It is practically a universal situation that the money received from the sale of the crop is the man's income" (Allen 1933, p. 147). She uses this to support her argument that, even though black women worked in the fields alongside their husbands, their husbands controlled the income from farm labor. Mann's article examines how the transition from slavery to sharecropping affected the position of freed Black women in the American South.

Finally, Carolyn E. Sachs in her book, *The Invisible Farmers: Women in Agricultural Production* references the same work by Allen. Sachs writes, "Her discussion of white women's work is insightful despite the fact that her description of black women's work is a racist interpretation." (Sachs, 1983, p. 25). She could be taking the position that any interpretation of the work of black women by a white woman will contain elements of racism, but she seems to be implying more than that racism is a relative term. She seems to be arguing that Allen's writing is racist in an absolute sense. That criticism does not seem justified in light of Ruth Allen's sensitivity to race not only in her study of the women cotton workers but in her later research as well, and in the way she lived her life, particularly her teaching at Huston-Tillotson College.[7] In a relative sense, we believe that Allen shows herself to be racially sensitive to an extent that was probably unusual for her time. She was writing in the early 1930's and although it is true that some of her observations may raise the eyebrows of a reader sixty years later, they should be interpreted in their historical context.

At the end of her chapter on "The Negro Woman" Allen writes,

> The comparatively large number of deserted wives who seem permanently deserted, and of unmarried mothers made the group seem rather depressing. This may however be due to the mental attitudes and social traditions of the interviewer (Allen 1933, pp. 287-288).

Rather than being judgmental, she attempts to qualify her observation on the basis of her own values and social background. One wonders what bothers Sachs so much. Unfortunately she does not explain what she finds racist in Allen's description of black women's labor. Perhaps she is referring to Allen's hypothesis as to why Negroes did not live as transient casual laborers in the same way that whites did? Allen writes,

> Unquestionably, one psychological factor of some force is the often noticed fear that the Negro seems to have of fresh air. He has never been accustomed to living in the open, and to be a true casual one must hear the call of the open road as a call of the blood (Allen 1933, p. 193).

Is this racist? Allen immediately follows this with,

> The bitter contempt which the settled Negro shows for the white folks who bring up their children on the road is a serious blow to any smugness of Nordic supremacy (Allen 1933, p. 193).

She goes on to explain that past experience with racism has made the Negro wary of traveling to unknown places.

> Further, the Negro is limited territorially by racial prejudice.........
> When the Negro has a place and knows that he is wanted, his natural inclination is to stay there (Allen 1933, p. 193).

Is this racist? We think not. Allen is simply drawing out the relationship between institutional constraints (habit, prejudice) and a particular group's behavior.

From the interest shown by these recent authors, we can conclude that Ruth Allen's work continues to have relevance up to sixty years after her first major piece of research was completed—quite a legacy. Looking to the broader influences of her work, we can discern two distinct themes: her analysis of family and gender relations vis-a-vis labor markets, and her efforts to leave an historical record of issues pertaining to the southwest's labor history. In the first case, Allen's work qualifies her as one of the first, along with women like Margaret Reid and Charlotte Perkins Gilman, to place women's production at the center of economic analysis. In the second case, Allen's rather unglamorous and painstaking compilation of historical information, while not containing much analytical insight in and of itself, has preserved an important record of the southwest's labor history from which researchers continue to draw today.

NOTES

1. Much of the material in this section is drawn from an unpublished paper by Forest Hill, "The Economics of Ruth Allen", n.d.

2. See Wendell Gordon, Forest Hill and C. Patton Blair, "In Memorium: Ruth Alice Allen", *Documents and Minutes of the General Faculty*, University of Texas at Austin, n.d.

3. For a more detailed account of the Texas School of Economics see Phillips (1989).

4. Throughout this paper we follow Allen's terminology regarding racial/ethnic classifications.

5.   Apparently, Allen netted out the production of women who were working solely for their families; this, we think, accounts for the seeming discrepancy in the numbers in this section.

6.   Allen has also been referenced relatively recently for her historical/ archival work. Articles in several historical journals, for example, have cited *East Texas Lumber Workers* and *The Great Southwest Strike* as overviews of their respective subjects. It seems, then, that these works have fulfilled Allen's hope that they serve as historical documents for future researchers.

7.   Personal accounts from two of her former students reveal Allen to have had an uncommon sensitivity to and awareness of racial issues, both relative to her era and in an absolute sense.

Chapter 6

Alton Wiley:
The Most Complete Economist

Gerald F. Vaughn

Agricultural economist Clarence A. Wiley, known by his middle
name Alton, was "the most complete economist among those
teaching in the department at that time" in depth of knowledge
encompassing the widest range of economic subfields. So states
Stephen L. McDonald, Emeritus Professor of Economics at the
University of Texas (McDonald, 1993a). McDonald came into the
University of Texas department of economics as a graduate
student in 1947, completed his master's thesis under Ayres in 1948
and doctoral dissertation under Wiley in 1951, and had been on
the faculty for several years at the time of Wiley's death in 1956.
Who was this agricultural economist Wiley? What was his
training, what were the sources of his institutionalism, and what
are his contributions to institutionalist thought and the solving
of society's problems? What is his legacy?

I. AS A RURAL YOUTH AND STUDENT AT
THE UNIVERSITIES OF TEXAS AND CHICAGO

Wiley was born on a ranch at the eastern edge of the Edwards
Plateau range country in Blanco County, Texas,

February 23, 1890, a son of William A. and Lena (Klett) Wiley. The Edwards Plateau was a unique ranching area since cattle, sheep, and goats were commonly grazed on the same ranch (the sheep for wool and goats for mohair). Also, ranches were fully-fenced. Small acreages of feed grains were grown to produce supplemental feed for livestock. The main cash crops in Wiley's immediate area were cotton and pecans.

Wiley was educated first in rural schools of Blanco County, then graduated from Johnson City High School in 1908. He taught in rural schools in Blanco, Runnels, and Williamson counties beginning in 1908 and worked on the ranch during the summers. In 1914 he received a diploma from Southwest Texas State Teachers (Normal) College at San Marcos and was appointed high school principal in Thrall, Texas, for the school years 1914-1915 and 1915-1916.

Improving education in the public schools of Texas remained a lifelong commitment for Wiley even after he became a university professor. He served on the State Executive Committee of the University Interscholastic League, an organization administered through the University of Texas for educational and sports competition in the public schools, for more than 20 years (1931-1935 and from 1937 until his death in 1956) (Bedichek 1956, p. 473).

In 1916-1917 Wiley worked as a bank teller in Taylor, Texas. In the school year 1917-1918, he was superintendent of the Florence, Texas, public schools. During World War I, from May 16, 1918, until discharge on March 30, 1919, he served as a private in the 36th Division, 131st Field Artillery, American Expeditionary Forces, which took him to the battlefields of France.

In Austin on April 2, 1919, Wiley married Effie Lee Wells of Salado, also a teacher; she was born in 1894 and died in 1982. They had three children, Gerald Alton (born 1924), Frances Elaine (1925-1982), and Joe Morris Wiley (born 1929).

In physical stature, Wiley was a man standing about six feet tall and at 165 pounds was slim most of his adult life. In his 60s his weight increased to perhaps 200 pounds. He wore glasses and had brown hair that grayed as he grew older. Throughout

Wiley's life, he was an avid hunter and fisherman. He also became an accomplished story-teller.

II. THE UNIVERSITY OF TEXAS

Beginning in the summer of 1914, Wiley sought higher education at the University of Texas, sometimes financing his studies by road work and part-time teaching. He loved to debate and wanted to become a lawyer; but his interest and career objective changed when he started taking economics courses (Wiley, Joe M., 1992-1993). In 1920, at the end of summer school, he received his bachelor's degree in Economics, Government, and History.

The first course Wiley took in the problems of rural America, to the solving of which he would devote his career, was *Rural Sociology* taught by A. C. Burkholder in summer school of 1920. Burkholder was a professor of rural education and sociology at Southwest Texas State Normal College, teaching at the University of Texas for the summer. His course description suggests he offered a fine understanding of rural problems:

> *Rural Sociology.*—A study of the social and economic phases of rural life in the United States, and especially in Texas, which seeks to discover what conditions actually exist, to set up standards worthy to be attained, and to propose means for their attainment. Some topics for special study are: Distinction between urban and rural; rural and urban increase; advantages and disadvantages of rural life; rural health, physical, mental, and moral; mental characteristics of the country man; rural credit; social aspects of land tenure and labor; inherent rights of the land worker; socialization of rural institutions; rural charity and correction. The attitude toward all phases of rural life will be sympathetic, but dynamic and constructive (University of Texas, 1920, pp. 28-29).

Continuing his studies in economics, history, and government, Wiley pursued his master's degree while also working as a tutor at the university. He received the M.A. degree in 1921, and his master's thesis was titled "Criticism of J. B. Clark's Specific Productivity Theory of Distribution."

Albert Benedict Wolfe was the supervisor of Wiley's thesis and probably influenced Wiley in the institutionalist direction. Wolfe came to the economics faculty of the University of Texas in 1914. His 1923 book, *Conservatism, Radicalism, and Scientific Method: An Essay on Social Attitudes*, reveals the substantial influence of Thorstein Veblen on his thought. In the academic year 1919-1920, Wiley took Wolfe's courses in *The Distribution of Wealth and Income* and *Industrial Reconstruction*. Wolfe also taught a stimulating course in *Social Problems*, which Wiley took the following year.

Wolfe's course in *Social Problems* must have been especially broadening to Wiley and the other students. The textbook presumably was Wolfe's 800-page *Readings in Social Problems*. His book was divided into five major sections: I. Problems of Population; II. Immigration; III. The Woman Problem; IV. Marriage and Divorce; and V. The Negro Problem in the United States. Wolfe held an ethical philosophy of economics that helped to prepare Wiley as a normative economist:

> We view all things against some background and in some sort of perspective. We have some sort of philosophy of life as the background, and a set of attitudes which determine the perspective. Analysis of these backgrounds and attitudes (so far as they touch economics) always reveals their essential nature to be a theory or conception of the purpose or function of social or economic activity. That the theory is usually the result of tradition and habit, and is rarely definitely formulated, does not argue that it is not present—and present as a guide to conduct. We cannot see the full facts of economic life in their essential significance unless they are projected upon the ethical background of aim and purpose. Nor will seeing be much more than a sensuous exercise unless it be designed to function, sooner or later, as a guide to action. It follows that economics teaching will be relatively barren (from any large social-productivity point of view) unless it be kept in intimate touch with, indeed infused with, ethical considerations (Wolfe 1920, pp. 744-745).

III.   SUMMER SCHOOL AT THE UNIVERSITY OF CHICAGO

Upon completing his master's degree in 1921, Wiley enrolled at the University of Chicago for the second term of the summer quarter. At the University of Texas, Wiley had taken several courses in economics and sociology under W. M. W. Splawn and Max Handman, who had doctorates from the University of Chicago and like Wolfe had a strong orientation toward social problems. Splawn and/or Handman may have encouraged Wiley to study at Chicago in the summer of 1921.

In political economy Wiley studied *The State in Relation to Labor,* taught by Harry Alvin Millis who achieved renown as a labor economist. In history Wiley took the course *Economic and Social Problems in Nineteenth Century Europe* taught by William Ezra Lingelbach, longtime professor of modern European history (and later dean of the college of arts and sciences) at the University of Pennsylvania who was teaching at the University of Chicago for the summer. Additionally, Wiley was a visitor in the course *Introduction to Statistics* taught by James Alfred Field.

IV.   RESUMING STUDIES AT UT

Following his summer quarter at the University of Chicago, Wiley returned to the University of Texas and worked as an instructor in economics for the next two years. He also continued his studies, taking courses at UT in 1921 and 1922.

In the University of Texas summer school of 1922, Wiley took his first course in agricultural economics. This was *Economics of Agriculture* taught by William E. Garnett, professor of rural social science at Texas Agricultural and Mechanical College who was teaching at the University of Texas for the summer. Garnett obtained his Ph.D. in agricultural economics at the University of Wisconsin in 1921, though his interests were primarily in rural sociology. In the summer school course at UT, he presumably taught the principles of agricultural economics advanced by Henry C. Taylor of the University of Wisconsin, who founded the discipline of agricultural economics in the early years of this century. Garnett may have been influential in Wiley's decision to undertake doctoral study there.

V.   INTRODUCED TO THE INTEGRATED
ECONOMY AT THE UNIVERSITY OF WISCONSIN

Wiley spent the summer of 1923 and the 1923-1924 academic year completing coursework at the University of Wisconsin, then the leading center of instruction in institutional economics, for his Ph.D. in agricultural economics. He returned to the University of Texas as adjunct professor in 1924 and was promoted to associate professor in 1926 when he received his Ph.D. from the University of Wisconsin, with a dissertation titled "Agriculture and the Business Cycle Since 1920: A Study in the Post-War Disparity of Prices." In 1928 Wiley's dissertation won first honorable mention in the Chicago Trust Company's Triennial Research Prize Contest.

Richard T. Ely, one of the outstanding early institutional economists and organizers, had left the Johns Hopkins University in 1892 to come to the University of Wisconsin as Director of the new School of Economics, Political Science, and History, which opened in 1892-1893. He founded and built the economics department to teach the principles of institutional economics.

Ely, who did his own graduate study at German universities in the late 1870s, was one of the first economists to understand the tendencies toward integration of the aggregate economy. In 1884 he wrote:

> The nation in its economic life is an organism, of which individuals, families, groups, and even towns, cities, provinces, etc., in their economic life form parts....
> As civilization advances, exchanges multiply and dependence increases. The economic life of a civilized people is today a most delicate organism, which easily gets out of order, as is seen in constantly recurring crises. Certain parts of this organism then cease to operate satisfactorily, and it becomes apparent how essential to the life of the whole is the performance of the functions of all the parts (Ely 1884, pp. 49, 51).

In Ely's book *An Introduction to Political Economy* published in 1889, he treats political economy as a subfield of sociology and embraces the study of society as a functional whole:

> As a first step in the study of sociology, and in that branch of sociology called political economy, it must be clearly understood that society is an organism; that is to say, it is composed of interdependent parts performing functions essential to the life of the whole.
> ....It follows as a direct consequence of this that the division of society into economic classes with the wide-extended division of labor is one of the fundamental facts of modern economic life (Ely 1889, pp. 14, 26).

Ely's understanding of society as an organism must have pervaded the instruction in economics and agricultural economics at the University of Wisconsin, as reflected in William E. Garnett's bulletin *Some Socially Significant Rural Conditions*. Garnett stated as one of the bulletin's objectives: *"To impress the fact of the interdependence and interrelationships* of all aspects of society, and especially how progress in any one of the big social concerns... is promoted or retarded by the prevailing conditions and stage of development in all of the others" (Garnett 1923, p. 39). Garnett may have opened Wiley's mind to this concept even before Wiley went to the University of Wisconsin for doctoral study.

Wiley saw the potential for rural America in that integrated economy. His eventual distinctiveness as a university professor came as, extending Ely's concept, he taught his own students about economic integration.

In his autobiography Ely writes: "The industrial question which has overshadowed in importance all other questions is this: 'Is industrial evolution naturally leading to the domination of substantially all the great fields of industry by monopoly?'" (Ely 1938, p. 265). Wiley took Ely's course in *Monopolies and Trusts*. Ely had written a book of that title published in 1900, and the subject remained a concern to him throughout his life. Abuses of monopoly power were widespread and severely damaging to the American economy, which probably is the reason why even in the 1950s Alton Wiley told his students:

> We should not let business swallow up government. If necessary let government set up enterprise in competition with private enterprise (Evans n.d., p. 7).

Under Benjamin H. Hibbard, Wiley took *Advanced Agricultural Economics* in which recent works in English, German, and French were used (Wiley was proficient in each language). Under Hibbard he also took *Farmer Movements* and *Research*. History of Agricultural Production, Land Problems, and Farm Credit. Hibbard was head of the Department of Agricultural Economics from 1919 to 1932, president of the American Farm Economic Association in 1922, and a leading authority on land policies. He equally was an expert on the history and development of farm organizations and farmer movements, which became one of Wiley's main interests.

From George S. Wehrwein Wiley took the course *Outlines of Land Economics*. Long recognized as a keen scholar in land economics, Wehrwein became president of the American Farm Economic Association in 1942 and vice president of the American Society of Planning Officials in 1944. In 1922 Ely, Mary L. Shine, and Wehrwein published a three-volume mimeographed work titled *Outlines of Land Economics*, all or part of which presumably was the text for the course Wiley took. Volume I dealt with *Characteristics and Classification of Land*, Volume II, *Costs and Income in Land Utilization*, and Volume III, *Land Policies*.

As a textbook *Outlines of Land Economics* represented the state-of-the-art in land economics at that time. The principles of land economics that Wiley learned found application in countless ways throughout his career. Not only were his eventual major journal articles excellent applications of land economics, but McDonald recalls that Wiley's teaching of agricultural economics courses also was well-flavored with theories from land economics (McDonald, 1993a). According to McDonald, Wiley frequently called attention to Johann Heinrich von Thunen's location theory, written in 1826, which Wehrwein taught at the University of Wisconsin.

Other economics courses Wiley took at the University of Wisconsin included *Critics of the Classical Economists* and *The Austrian School and Recent Developments* taught by William A. Scott, also *Advanced Economics* taught by William H. Kiekhofer. In agricultural economics he took *Marketing Farm*

Products under Theodore Macklin. Outside the field of economics, he took the history course *Nineteenth Century Europe* taught by Joseph V. Fuller and the political science course *State Government in the United States* taught by Allan F. Saunders.

Wiley acquired several distinct characteristics of the University of Wisconsin's approach to institutional economics. Richard S. Kirkendall has identified four such characteristics of Ely and his associates:

> [First is] the historical approach that was a characteristic of Wisconsin's institutional economists. Three other Wisconsin characteristics [are]: the Turner thesis (the Frederick Jackson Turner view of the economic history of the American West and the relation of the frontier, free land, and democracy); the Progressive philosophy that the government needed to attack social and economic problems, including problems in the use of natural resources; and the idea that intellectuals should devote themselves to affairs of importance to people outside of the academy, serving in government offices when necessary (Kirkendall 1963, pp. 206-207).

VI. TEACHING AND REFINING THE CONCEPT OF THE INTEGRATED ECONOMY

Wiley was promoted to full professor by the University of Texas Board of Regents in 1929. His rapid rise from tutor in only eight years attests to the potential that colleagues and administrators saw in him. The final promotion came with astonishing speed. On August 28, 1929, Wiley wrote to Edmund T. Miller, head of the economics department, indicating he would not return to UT at his present rank and salary. Wiley pointed to past offers he had received carrying higher salaries and to his current negotiations with the Division of Land Economics of the U.S. Department of Agriculture, having been "interviewed by Dr. L. C. Gray, Chief of the Division, and asked if I would be available this year for the work" (Wiley 1929a).

Later that same day Miller, in a letter signed by full professors Robert H. Montgomery and George W. Stocking also, wrote to University of Texas president Harry Y.

Benedict requesting Wiley's promotion to full professor with a salary increase. Miller stated:

> Dr. Wiley has received during the past three years two offers from Oklahoma A.& M., one from the University of South Dakota, and one from Auburn, Ala. All paid more than he was receiving here. He never took advantage of these offers to get promotion here. He feels that he cannot continue to be so self denying, and unless he receives recognition now, he will leave us for the U.S. Department of Agriculture (Miller 1929).

On September 3rd, President Benedict wrote to Miller: "I am hereby approving to the Board of Regents your recommendation that Dr. C. A. Wiley be made a full Professor of Economics... effective September 15, 1929..." (Benedict 1929). Wiley also got the salary increase he asked for.

Wiley was preeminently a teacher even more than scholar. He taught a wide array of courses during his career, including non-agricultural economics courses such as Introduction to Economics, Principles of Economics, Economic Problems, and for many years Economic and Social Statistics. Agricultural economics had been taught only sporadically before, so we find in the academic year 1922-1923 he wrote in his Instructor's Report: "Procured the sources, worked up and organized course in agric. economics." He had 21 students, 15 men and 6 women, in his first course teaching in the specialty in which he gained distinction.

VI.   WILEY'S COURSES IN AGRICULTURAL AND LAND ECONOMICS

Wiley taught a succession of courses in agricultural and land economics over the years. Changes in course titles and descriptions reveal the progression of his thought and deeper understanding of maladjustments in the agricultural economy and readjustments needed to better integrate agriculture and rural America into the aggregate economy.

The description for Wiley's first agricultural economics course indicates his fine basic understanding of agricultural and land economics: *"Agricultural Economics.*—A study of land problems; farm equipment; the choice and combination of the factors of production; rents and profits; farm ownership; tenantry; and marketing of farm products" (University of Texas 1923, p. 145). After returning from doctoral study, Wiley changed the course description to: *"Agricultural Economics.*—A study of the development of the economic problems of a specialized agriculture; relation of agriculture to the general welfare; problems of production, prices and the standard of living; measures for agricultural relief, including the development of cooperative marketing; and general problems and policies in land utilization" (University of Texas 1926, p. 127).

By the mid-1930s, even prior to his work in the Roosevelt administration, Wiley's growing understanding of the agricultural economy caused him to divide his Agricultural Economics course into two courses. One was built on the first half of his former course and its description read: *"The Economic Background of Modern Agriculture.*—A study of the economic forces leading to the development of modern agriculture, dealing with the problems of self-sufficiency, its breakdown and the beginnings of the price system, the advent of commercialized agriculture, factors in balanced production, problems of diminishing returns, marketing, size of farms, the intensity of culture, and profitable agriculture." The other was built on the second half of his former course, with this description: *"Problems of Modern Agriculture.*—An analysis of the present-day ills of agriculture, with special emphasis upon the surplus problem, low purchasing power of agricultural products, and current proposals for reform. Attention is also given to problems of agricultural tariffs, taxation, transportation, land utilization, farm tenancy, and conservation programs of federal and state governments" (University of Texas 1935, p. 68).

As conditions changed during World War II, Wiley placed emphasis simply on maladjustments and needed readjustments.

Revised course descriptions read: *"Economic Background of Modern Agriculture.*—Economic implications of the transition from self-sufficient to commercialized agriculture; the merits of programs and policies in light of needed readjustments"; *"Problems of Modern Agriculture.*—The character and causes of maladjustments of modern agriculture; price problems; an evaluation of proposed readjustments" (University of Texas 1945, p. 104).

By 1949 Wiley saw the need to redivide his agricultural economics courses and the two became four, with further changes in focus and emphasis (University of Texas 1949, pp. 122-123). *Economic Background of Modern Agriculture* became: *"Evolution of Modern Agriculture.*—Production patterns in a self-sufficient agriculture; technological change and subsequent institutional mutations from feudal tenure to individual proprietorship; growth of agricultural maladjustments and unbalance." *Problems of Modern Agriculture* became: *"Agricultural Problems and Policies.*—Agriculture in a dynamic economy; long-run and cyclical aspects of maladjustments; appraisal of various support programs for agriculture; possible future policies." Two new courses were created: *"Survey of Modern Agriculture.*—Production patterns and problems presented by modern commercialized agriculture; its position in the economy, with implications of present trends; background for further problems analysis"; *"Economics of Farmer Movements.*—Analysis of agricultural discontent growing out of changed patterns in the economy; problems confronting agriculture; programs of farmers' organizations designed to bring relief."

Correlative to Wiley's agricultural economics courses were those he taught in agricultural finance and land economics, beginning in the 1920s. Changes in descriptions of these latter courses reveal changes he perceived in the major resource institutions of credit and property.

Wiley's course in agricultural finance began as: *"Agricultural Finance.*—Development of the financial needs of agriculture; classification of these needs for production and marketing; analysis of principles and practices prevailing among current agricultural credit institutions of this country and abroad. Special emphasis on methods of financing farm producers, home owners, and farmers' cooperative marketing and distributing organizations" (University of Texas 1927, p. 134). In 1939 the last sentence was dropped. In 1945 the course received this description: *"Agricultural Finance.*—The development of modern agriculture and its credit needs; deficiencies of early institutions serving agriculture, and the rise and functioning of federally-sponsored credit institutions serving agriculture" (University of Texas 1945, p. 104).

Wiley's course in land economics took shape as: *"Land Problems.*—A course dealing with the settlement of the national domain; the emergence of land problems; programs for land reform; the land question in foreign countries; present utilization of land; and policies suggested in regard to the future classification and utilization of land" (University of Texas 1926, p. 129). In 1939 the description changed to: *"Land Problems.*—Inventory of nation's land supply, land classification, and principles governing efficient land use. Attention given also to existing maladjustments and proposed programs of readjustment" (University of Texas 1939, p. 69). In later years, changes in course title were made without significant changes in description. In 1941 the course was retitled *Land Economics,* in 1945 *Land Policies,* and in 1949 *Land Problems* again. Course descriptions under the 1941 and succeeding titles continue to emphasize fundamentals of efficient land use, existing land use maladjustments, and programs of reform. Wiley placed emphasis on allocative efficiency in production as the objective of the integrated economy. He shared L. C. Gray's emphasis on efficient land use, no doubt instilled in them at the University of Wisconsin where both studied:

> ...Efficiency occupied a high place in Gray's scheme, although other values also influenced his views about the ways in which land should be used (Kirkendall 1963, p. 206).

VII.   CROSS-FERTILIZATION
OF IDEAS WITH AYRES

Wiley was 40 years old and Clarence E. Ayres slightly younger
when Ayres came into the UT economics department in 1930.
Both men had received outstanding training at the Ph.D. level.
Both were mature and independent thinkers, whose views of the
world probably were already well formed. It is unlikely that they
influenced each other's thinking greatly. Yet they got along well
together as colleagues, and I believe the following examples
suggest possible cross-fertilization of ideas between them.

In 1939 Wiley wrote a brilliant article titled "The Rust
Mechanical Cotton Picker and Probable Land-Use Adjustments" in the *Journal of Land and Public Utility Economics*.
Each new attempt at developing a successful mechanical cotton
picker caused near-hysteria at the fear that millions of cotton
field-workers in the South would be displaced and added to the
nation's mass of unemployed. In an excellent economic analysis,
which drew in part from his own experience in picking cotton,
Wiley discussed the technological, topographic, economic, and
institutional obstacles to adoption of a mechanical cotton picker
and showed why adoption would be slow in coming. Adoption
would accelerate only, he predicted, in this event:

> Were some economic forces introduced into the South, possibly more
> industrialization and a decreasing birth rate among the population,
> which would effect a better adjustment between the rural population
> and the land supply, thereby causing wages and standards of living to
> rise, mechanized cotton production would be forced in areas adapted
> to such methods... On the contrary, in the absence of forces external
> to cotton production tending to increase the wages of farm labor, it
> hardly seems logical to expect the machine to displace hand labor in
> picking unless it can show greater economies than are now in sight
> .... Probably an upset of this character is essential to the reconstruction
> of the cotton economy of the South, with its attendant evils of misery,
> poverty, ignorance, and poor health. However, the initial blow to break
> the vicious circle of ignorance and poverty must be delivered by public
> authority in the interest of social welfare where physical conditions and
> standards of living offer private enterprise no economic incentive for
> doing so. At present, no existing social program for the South gives

promise of hastening the process. In view of the grip of 'agrarian' influences on policy makers, the trend seems tending in the other direction (Wiley 1939, pp. 162, 164).

Wiley's prediction proved correct, and indeed it took World War II to hasten the process. So many field-workers never returned to those cotton fields after leaving for military service or work in wartime industries that cotton growers faced labor shortages and high wage costs, hence the incentive to move more quickly toward mechanized harvesting.

Wiley's article was published five years before Ayres' book *The Theory of Economic Progress*, which comprehensively examines the interrelationships between institutions and technology. Wiley's article anticipates Ayres' definitive work on institutional rigidity as it inhibits technological and economic progress. Assuming Ayres read Wiley's article, it may have contributed to Ayres' theory.

Wiley saw the multi-sector causes and effects of what seemed a single exogenous change and understood them within the framework of the entire national economy:

> He saw that the picker could not displace hand labor unless accompanied by growth of off-farm opportunities for poor farm workers, the blocking up of larger farm units, and a shift of cotton production from the upland South to the level lands of the Mississippi delta and the Southwest...
>
> It is this understanding of the interrelatedness of all parts of the economy that distinguishes Wiley's thinking on farm problems. What we call farm problems, he would say, are really symptoms of a larger problem: the occupational immobility of farm labor exacerbated by massive unemployment in the nonfarm sectors. He felt that the isolation of the farm population from the culture and market relations of urban life, perpetuating a different 'way of life' and a different way of thinking, also produced an institutional barrier to occupational mobility—a barrier that the agrarian 'solution' raised still higher...Thus in his classes he spoke of the need to 'integrate' the agricultural sector with the rest of the economy (McDonald 1992a).

A simple measure of the degree to which the agricultural sector was disconnected from the rest of the economy and society is the percentage of farms having telephones and electricity. In 1930 only 25 percent of U.S. farms had telephones and 13 percent had electricity. In 1940 only 34 percent had telephones and 33 percent had electricity. By 1954, shortly before Wiley's death, still only 49 percent of all farms had telephones, though 93 percent had electricity.

Ayres saw technology as instrumental in creating value and as the scientifically measurable or objective basis of the theory of value. Therefore he held that the instrumental theory of value was superior to, and should replace or at least take precedence over, the subjective price theory of value. Most economists trained in neoclassical price theory reacted so negatively to Ayres' proposal that they found little if any use for his instrumental theory of value. Unfortunately this caused them to also ignore Ayres' deeper understanding of the role of technology in economic development.

Wiley never lost sight of Ayres' overarching theme of the significance of technology in economic development, and he applied Ayres' instrumental theory of value (properly, in my judgment) as supplementing or complementing, rather than in any sense replacing, the price theory of value. The relation between the instrumental and price theories of value really is a both/and, not an either/or, relation. There is much about human behavior and economic life that is subjective and always will be.

Cross-fertilization of ideas between Wiley and Ayres on the instrumental theory of value is further suggested by an intriguing paper written by J. Fagg Foster in 1942, titled "The Approach to Land Use Planning in a Changing Technology." In addition to his coursework with Ayres, Foster took Wiley's courses *Problems of Modern Agriculture* (summer session 1937) and *Land Problems* (summer session 1938).

Foster's paper was published in 1981 in the *Journal of Economic Issues* among a collection of his previously unpublished papers, and in the editor's introduction Baldwin Ranson observed:

The last five papers have been applications of parts of Foster's reconstruction in economics. But they have been suggestive rather than extensive, detailed, and empirically based tests of that reconstruction. Among his papers is but one that provides such extended application and test. It was written in 1942, so the data on which it is based are not current. But it still appears valuable in helping modern readers evaluate the significance of Foster's contribution to economic analysis (Foster 1981, p. 985).

While the instrumental theory of value became an organizing view for the teaching and writing of not only Ayres but also some of his institutionalist colleagues in the economics department, Ayres himself was able to give his theory of value only limited application to problems of the real world. It remained for colleagues, principally Wiley and Erich W. Zimmermann, to give the theory real-world meaning. Without their practical applications of the technological continuum to solving agricultural and land problems and the development of world resources and industries, Ayres' theory would have had little meaning and even less acceptance.

Foster attempted the synthesis of Ayres' theory with Wiley's practical concerns for public policy on agriculture and land problems, and the attempt was fairly successful. Foster traces the institutional and technological evolution of agriculture, then addresses the difficult problem of how to adjust agricultural land use in a changing technology. He offers three principles of effective land use planning: (1) Technological determination, (2) recognized interdependence, and (3) minimum dislocation.

Foster's first principle is grounded in Ayres' instrumentalism and says that land should be used for the welfare of society in accordance with technological and economic efficiency, though Foster may have been overly optimistic about the ease with which technological and economic efficiency of land use can be determined. His second principle essentially says that land use planning will not have support and be effective unless the people affected recognize their interdependence and understand that land use planning is for the common good. His third principle holds that land use planning will not have support and be effective unless disruption of people's lives is kept to a

tolerable minimum. The second and third principles are
grounded in Wiley's land use planning experience with the
Resettlement Administration in the Southeast.

It is unfortunate that Foster's paper was not written and
published earlier, when it could have contributed to the
agricultural and land policy debate prior to World War II.
Nonetheless, it offers valuable guidance for land use planning
of many kinds, even today.

Another interesting example of cross-fertilization between
Wiley and Ayres is a master's thesis titled "Application of the
Instrumental Theory of Value to Agricultural Economics,"
written by Elgin Williams under Wiley's supervision in 1944
(the thesis is incorrectly listed under E. (Edward) Williams in
the University of Texas library catalog). Ayres was a member
of Williams' thesis committee. Most of the thesis explains the
instrumental theory of value, building toward "a review of some
standard introductory texts in agricultural economics, which are
criticized in Ayresian terms for their agrarian attitudes and
association of 'value' with utility and limited resources"
(McDonald 1993b). Williams asserts:

> We have seen that the instrumental theory finds value to be the
> continuity of the technological process.... To put this principle in
> another way: All agricultural policy proposals must answer to the
> questions 'What would be the effect of this action on the technological
> process? Would it impede or release full application of existing and new
> techniques? Would it destroy or bolster institutional inhibitions to
> technology? Does the statement of the proposal itself imply other criteria
> than the instrumental?' (Williams 1944, pp. 89, 108).

Bert M. Evans took three of Wiley's courses, *The Evolution
of Modern Agriculture, Economics of Farmer Movements,* and
Agricultural Problems and Policies, in 1953-1954 while
studying for his master's degree before going to Harvard
University for the Ph.D. His master's thesis under Wiley was
titled "Institutional Inhibitors to Adequate Farm Size
Adjustments." Ayres was on Evans' committee, and the thesis
is another example of likely cross-fertilization of ideas between
Wiley and Ayres. Evans wrote:

The ultimate value concept upon which this analysis of the institutional factors that inhibit progress toward an economic sized functionally producing farm unit is based is that of science and technology. Consistency with the technological continuum is assumed to be the basis for judgement of social objectives. If a moral end-in-view consistent with the technological continuum is necessary, the writer assumes that our economic system functions with the foreseeable objective of providing more goods, services, and leisure time for a greater number of people. Thus, an objective of the functionally producing farm, as a part of an integrated agricultural sector, is to contribute to that end....

The economic system of the present is technologically motivated and economic value should be based on the technological instrumentality of our economic endeavors rather than on the mores developed to reconcile actualities of living in a past technologically inferior situation (Evans 1954, pp. 119, 122-123).

Jean Richardson, retired President of Del Mar College, did his doctoral dissertation under Wiley and recalls that:

The essence of Dr. Wiley's approach was that agriculture was an industry devoted to the production of foods and fibers and it should be examined objectively in terms of how effectively it achieved this purpose...To Wiley, too often agricultural policy had confused the preservation of a way of life with the promotion of efficiency in production of foods and fibers... (Richardson 1992a).

To Wiley the core problem for farm policy had three facets, in Evans' words:

(1) A tendency toward the underemployment of the human resources applied to agricultural production.

(2) The failure of the agricultural sector to become adequately integrated into the changing industrial system.

(3) The lack of a balanced economy with implications for agricultural adjustment (Evans n.d., p. 6).

Wiley felt that maladjustments should be analyzed "on the basis of institutionalist theory" and policy and program is a matter of "replacing maladjustments with readjustments." He felt that all national policies and programs "have implications for agricultural adjustment—negative or positive—and they should be modified to have a positive effect." This would result in "integrating the agricultural sector into the total economy in a comprehensive fashion over time" (Evans n.d., pp. 6-7).

The end state in Wiley's concept of total, perfect, or complete integration of the aggregate economy may be captured by his eventual use of the term *fusion*. Evans writes:

> 'Fusion' was a frequently used concept. Professor Wiley explained 'fusion' as the merging of separate economies into a larger whole. He very carefully distinguished this from what others might interpret as aggregation. 'Fusion' brought about an entirely different economy or economic activity. Thus, it was a prime process in the evolution away from established custom. It made for placing a 'premium on non-conformity' as opposed to conformity (Evans n.d., pp. 3-4).

Ayres' writing that is directed most specifically to economic integration, with implications for fusion, is a chapter in a book of essays honoring philosophy professor Max Otto and published in 1952. Ayres suggests that maximum integration is achieved at "full production" in the sense of "full use of the 'industrial potential'" (Ayres 1952b, pp. 175-176). Ayres indicates that industrial potential "is knowable" and "subject to fairly precise measurement"; moreover, it is "well within our powers to enlarge—as witness the tremendous enlargement of the American industrial potential during the recent war" (Ayres 1952b, p. 177).

McDonald was a student of Ayres and learned much from him. Ayres served on the committee for McDonald's dissertation "Future Agricultural Policy with a View To an Integrated Economy" completed under Wiley in 1951. Presumably here too was a cross-fertilization of ideas between Wiley and Ayres.

Ayres' thinking as expressed in 1952 is generally consistent with McDonald's and differs only to the extent that Ayres seemed to feel the process of economic integration in the United States was advancing more rapidly than McDonald did. Ayres felt that the demonstrable cause-and-effect relationship between curtailment of production and curtailment of employment in the Depression of the 1930s, followed immediately by their complete reversal as America went :nto full production and full employment during World War II, once and for all time convinced everyone that prosperity depends on full production.

Prior to the Depression, and in fact contributing to its onset, big business routinely cut back production to create scarcity and thereby raise prices and profits (or at least assure solvency). This was the dichotomy or dualism that Ayres and Veblen before him observed, by which industrial (technological) efficiency was sought on the one hand while competitive financial (pecuniary) strategy dictated otherwise. Ayres was convinced that the experiences of the Depression and World War II put America well along the road toward eliminating that dichotomy, which had been a deep cleavage in our culture, and to him the proof of rapidly progressing integration could be seen in the maintenance of full production from the end of the war to the time of his chapter's publication in 1952. Though Ayres did not use the term fusion, complete elimination of the dichotomy would essentially produce fusion or the end-state of the integrated economy. Recessions in the late 1950s and repeatedly since then make it clear that Ayres was overly optimistic. McDonald's dissertation did not anticipate such rapid progress, especially with a major sector such as agriculture still largely outside the orb of integration.

Wiley's concept of fusion builds on, then extends beyond, use of the term in economic anthropology. Neil J. Smelser refers to "the continuum from structural fusion to structural differentiation" and indicates that "family-production fusion" is characteristic of an undifferentiated social structure and underdeveloped economy (Smelser 1967, pp. 34-35). Differentiation "characterizes a social structure moving toward greater complexity," integration "in certain respects balances the divisive character of differentiation," and social disturbances "result from the discontinuities between differentiation and integration" (Smelser 1967, p. 48). However, Smelser makes clear:

> ...Even though the forces of differentiation, integration, and disturbances are closely linked empirically, we should not 'close' the 'system' composed of the relationship among the three forces. Differentiation may arise from sources other than economic

development; the requirement of integration may arise from conditions
other than differentiation; and the sources of social disturbance are not
exhausted by the discontinuities between differentiation and integration
(Smelser 1967, p. 48).

Wiley's concept of fusion implies that integration (really
reintegration) of a differentiated complex social structure and
developed economy can progress from one form of fusion to
another, from the level of simple family-production fusion to
the level of some higher form of fusion. In other words, the
continuum extends not merely from structural fusion to
structural differentiation but leads on to structural fusion in a
new form.

VIII. EARLY SCHOLARSHIP: EXAMINING PROBLEMS AND ISSUES OF RURAL AMERICA

As a scholar Wiley came to prominence in 1930 when his
updated dissertation was published as a book of the same title
(*Agriculture and the Business Cycle Since 1920...*). In the book's
preface, he acknowledges University of Wisconsin agricultural
economics professors Hibbard and Macklin "for stimulating an
immediate interest in the farm price problem" (Wiley 1930, p.
vii). He also acknowledges economics professors Kiekhofer and
Scott as "an important source of inspiration through their
teachings in the field of economic theory and history of
economic thought, respectively."

Wiley's book was a probing analysis of international supply,
demand, and world trade factors, or transactional flows,
affecting the competitive position of United States agriculture
in the aftermath of World War I. The research approach was
a positive rather than normative study, though Wiley became
a more normative economist later in life.

Wiley understood and taught reciprocity as central to his
concept of the integration of agriculture into the aggregate
economy. Once agriculture has advanced so that the basic food
and fiber needs of society can be consistently met, other

industries arise and reciprocity begins. Were reciprocity not possible between other industries and agriculture, farmers could not obtain the industrial technology that enables more efficient agricultural production. This in turn frees more agricultural resources (land, labor, capital, and management) to produce goods and services apart from food and fiber and contributes to the continuing shift of population from rural to urban areas. The nonfarm economy is thereby strengthened, which makes possible further reciprocity with agriculture. Reciprocity like world trade flourishes with full employment, capacity output, and prosperity, and in times of economic depression both reciprocity and world trade are diminished. Wiley observed:

> Over and above the minimum necessities to sustain life, the total demand for the products of a given industry is composed of the offerings of other commodities in exchange on an equitable basis. Prerequisites to the existence of a maximum demand for the products of all industries are, (1) balanced production, and (2) the smooth operation of the machinery of exchange. These essentials are the culmination of years of adjustment in production, along with the building up of contacts with markets, the establishment of credit relationships and stability of the standard of value. Post-war economic and political conditions ran counter to each of these essentials; production was thrown out of adjustment, old markets were demoralized, new ones either starved or were glutted, credits were curtailed, and stability of the standards of value was a myth. .... The decreased industrial production had unmeshed the machinery of exchange.
> .... The rebuilding of industry and commerce means the rebuilding and replacement of human relationships in the channels of trade, credit, transportation, and a hundred other ways, which were built up only after long years of painstaking effort. Neither can those relationships be restored within a few months, or even years, merely because the wish is father to the thought (Wiley 1930, pp. 81, 83, 116).

Price stabilization was the paramount concern of Wiley and most other agricultural economists throughout the 1920s and early 1930s. As the Depression of the 1930s deepened between 1929 and 1932, prices of goods and services that U.S. farmers bought declined 32 percent but prices that farmers received fell more than 50 percent. In 1932 realized net farm income was less than one-third of what it was in 1929.

Wiley felt that with agriculture's low elasticity of demand (both price-and income-inelastic) for its products, national farm income could not increase enough to support all the families then engaged in farming. In a previous article, he said "the surest path to the farmer's prosperity is through curtailment of production by reducing the number of farmers, thereby giving each the benefits of volume of production at high prices, rather than through individual farm curtailment which would result in higher prices for a lower volume of production with operating charges remaining practically fixed, however" (Wiley 1925-26, p. 348).

Wiley could urge farmers to take off-farm jobs when employment opportunities existed, in the mid-1920s and again in the 1940s and 50s. But in 1930 and throughout the Depression, an era of massive unemployment, encouraging farmers to leave agriculture for off-farm jobs would have been unreasonable and futile. His book did not make a case for reducing the number of farmers, except to suggest that government aid could take the form of:

> ...preferential credit and assistance in marketing, restriction upon the number of farmers, or in the curtailment of individual farm operations through some scheme of taxation of producers, of arbitrary supervision of their productive efforts (Wiley 1930, p. 225).

Since individual farmers, farm cooperatives, and the limited governmental intervention then operative were unable to keep supply in balance with demand, the task of controlling production to improve farm prices required stronger governmental intervention. In 1932 Wiley's book was reviewed favorably, though not uncritically, by Mordecai Ezekiel and Oris V. Wells, two key participants in the subsequent drafting of New Deal farm legislation (see reference note for Wiley 1930).

Wiley felt that "measures for temporary relief of agriculture must differ materially from permanent policies" (Wiley 1930, p. 348). He was sympathetic to New Deal emergency farm relief measures...though in full recognition that the long-term solution to low farm income was to enable more farm families to obtain jobs in the non-farm economy as it improved. Presumably he supported passage of the Agricultural Adjustment Act in 1933. A master's thesis titled "The Administrative Set-Up of the A. A. A.," completed by Annie Bettie M. Armstrong in 1934 under Wiley's supervision, has a hopeful rather than critical tone. The Act's primary objective was to "relieve the existing national economic emergency by increasing agricultural purchasing power" (quoted in Armstrong 1934, p. 1), which was very much in line with Wiley's thinking about the integrated economy as expressed in his book.

As soon as the Depression crisis began to ease, Wiley again could urge reduction in the number of farmers... which he continued for the rest of his life. The idea of encouraging and enabling farmers to leave agriculture was not well received by many agricultural economists and others in his lifetime. It has since proven to be exactly the right adjustment.

Wiley's book also contains some revealing insights about his approach to economic research. In his study of agricultural price disparity:

> ...*causes* receive more attention than *effects*. It is not essential that precise measurements of the *effects* be registered in order to obtain a thorough diagnosis of *causes*. The degree of fever registered by a patient bears only a remote relation to the diagnosis of the precise causes of his illness...[The disparity to be explained] is one of causes, not of effects; one of direction and character, not of degree (Wiley 1930, pp. iii-v).

Determining the causes was guided by this institutional economics framework:

> With these principles in mind, certain factors have been discussed as having contributed to the production of a relative over-supply of farm products; others as having lessened the effective demand for these products. These factors, in some cases, have been 'natural,' while in others they have been 'artificial' or man-made. But 'natural' here is to be interpreted to apply only to weather and climatic forces, and not to any so-called 'natural law of supply and demand.' The 'artificial' forces are the results of economic philosophy and institutional arrangements, rather than of a 'natural' economic order. Much political action and governmental policy—national and international—have been

examined and their results listed, accordingly, as a supply or a demand
factor in the agricultural situation.

On the basis of whether these factors affect the demand or the supply,
they are classified according to *effect*. On the other hand, the
classification depending upon whether these factors are 'natural' or
'artificial' is based upon *origin*. In the task of explaining the causes of
the agricultural depression, the origin of any *supply* or *demand*
influence, or how it might have been avoided, is of less significance than
the direction of its effect. However, the origin of these factors may
become of great significance presently in the question of adjustment and
measures for reform.

.... Economic forces are largely *institutional*, and, consequently,
'artificial,' rather than 'natural.'

.... The idea is to emphasize that economic situations are the result,
largely, of factors not 'natural,' but 'artificial,' and therefore alterable
and remediable (Wiley 1930, pp. 195-196, 221, 224).

Wiley's view of the analytical role of the economist was further
expressed:

It is true, the economist does contend that a decreased price, relatively,
is accompanied by a decreased supply. In a general way, everyone knows
as much—even a parrot, when asked, 'What determines price?' can be
taught to say, 'Demand and supply.' But the economist goes further and
attempts more than this; he analyzes; he differentiates. He does not
proclaim, in any case, an instantaneous adjustment as if wrought by
magic. Time is an element in any adjustment, and the amount varies
with industries, as well as with economic conditions and governmental
'influence.' Above everything else, the economist emphasizes the
differences between immediate and long-run effects (Wiley 1930, p. 207).

IX.   CROSS-FERTILIZATION OF
IDEAS WITH DR. BOB

Montgomery, known affectionately as Dr. Bob, was Wiley's
closest friend in the economics department and probably knew
Wiley better than anyone else there (Richardson, 1992b). They
had much in common. They were almost the same age, and both
were born in rural Blanco County. Both attended Southwest
Texas State Normal School and started out as teachers in the
public schools. Both served in the U.S. Army in World War I.

Montgomery obtained his master's degree in economics at the University of Texas when Wiley was an instructor in the department. They were promoted to full professor at UT within a year of each other. Each viewed economics as a normative science and worked for the New Deal during the Depression. They understood the problems of agriculture and rural people, also the need to regulate industry and utilities.

Wiley became an expert in agricultural and land economics and Montgomery an expert in corporation finance and public utility economics, yet each could and did work in the other's field of specialization. Montgomery's Ph.D. dissertation was a study of the law of cooperative farm marketing associations, he taught the UT course in agricultural cooperatives, and he assisted cotton cooperatives in Texas for many years; he also spoke to farm groups to help them understand the New Deal farm programs. Wiley had taken Splawn's course in *Public Utilities* as a graduate student at the University of Texas and later Ely's course in *Monopolies and Trusts*; also, the land economics course Wiley took under Wehrwein dealt with public utility land among its topics. This together with his other economics training and experience in land economics qualified Wiley to testify before a Texas legislative committee investigating public utilities.

Montgomery and Wiley shared (as did Ayres) an appreciation for cultural anthropology. Dr. Bob and Alton agreed about the role of technology in resource utilization and in shaping institutional and cultural change, and they shared a common understanding of the factors instrumental in economic development of the American frontier.

In short, Montgomery and Wiley tended to see things alike, and each probably influenced and/or reinforced the other's thinking in important respects. Montgomery was knowledgeable, for instance, about farm tenancy and contributed to the conduct of Wiley's major research project on farm ownership and tenancy in Texas under the Laura Spelman Rockefeller grant. Similarly, Wiley was well trained in marginal analysis (including the Austrian school of marginalist thought) and doubtless supported Montgomery's pioneering efforts to encourage railroads and electric utilities to use marginal cost as the basis for rate-setting in situations of decreasing costs.

An example of cross-fertilization of ideas between Montgomery and Wiley is seen in the doctoral dissertation of Claiborne Alexander Duval completed in 1932. Wiley supervised it and Montgomery was on the committee. Duval's dissertation was titled "Basic Farm Reform," and it was an intriguing exercise in economic planning whereby Duval proposed an approach to farm price stabilization within a band or corridor so as to be fair to both producers and consumers. His plan proposed "to keep the marginal cost and the market price close together" (Duval 1932, pp. iii-iv).

Duval described his dissertation as "a study of the farm problem from the point of view of an economic engineer." He defined an economic engineer as "a person, or a group of persons, who takes the information furnished by the science of economics and uses this information to design, repair, control, or operate an entire economic system." In his acknowledgments, Duval thanks Montgomery for "the viewpoint of an economic engineer, for a thorough training in the problems of corporation finance and public utilities, and above all for enthusiasm and encouragement when the writer was most discouraged..." McDonald observes: "Montgomery was on the committee, and I sense more of him than of Wiley in the argument and its form" (McDonald 1993b). Montgomery's clear interest in Duval's work is reflected by his referring to it in a published paper on the problems of cotton growers given at the American Institute of Cooperation summer session of 1931:

> Several attempts have been made by statisticians to rule out all other relevant forces and to measure mathematically the relationships between price changes and plantings, and between production and price changes. The best work along this line that has come to my attention is an unpublished manuscript by Mr. C. A. Duval of the University of Texas (Montgomery 1931a, p. 204).

X. WILEY'S DEFINING EXPERIENCE IN THE NEW DEAL

Wiley's focus on the integrated economy, and the social planning and control needed for its recovery as the Depression deepened, also is reflected in the Duval dissertation. Duval understood that: "In an exchange economy no one economic problem can be solved alone" (Duval 1932, p. iii). He indicated the economic principles that guided his proposed economic reform:

> The first principle is that division of labor in all of its forms tends to increase the efficiency of man in the physical production of goods and services. The second principle is that the best balance in production between producer and consumer can be secured only by adjusting the factors of production in accordance with the various laws of diminishing returns. The third principle is that a system of conscious economic control is essential before the best balance in production can be secured. The fourth principle is that so called 'human nature,' or 'human motivation,' in so far as it affects economic behavior, is primarily the result of social heritage or social attitudes, which are themselves amenable to conscious social control (Duval 1932, p. 6).

Wiley's defining experience came in the mid-1930s when he took a leave of absence from his post at the University of Texas to serve in the New Deal administration of President Franklin D. Roosevelt, confronting the grave and interrelated problems of land utilization and farm tenancy. Here was Wiley's opportunity to apply economic theory and social reforms to real-world problems on a large scale; the experience reshaped his thinking.

Wiley's view as of early 1935, while sensitive to the ignorance and poverty associated with the plight of tenants and sharecroppers, seems to reflect the situation as he knew it in the Southwest where the problem was somewhat less severe than that in the Southeast. His subsequent work for the Resettlement Administration in trying to alleviate the poverty and deprivation of hundreds of thousands of rural people in Alabama, Georgia, Florida, and South Carolina, and even his brief earlier experience with rural rehabilitation in Texas, were shocking and life-changing. He was exposed to conditions of life so stark as to be unimaginable. These were the conditions of which the famous book *Let Us Now Praise Famous Men* by James Agee and Walker Evans, a study of three tenant families in Alabama in 1936 when Wiley was headquartered there, is so graphically and eloquently descriptive (Agee and Evans 1941).

XI.   RURAL REHABILITATION IN TEXAS

Wiley's willingness to work toward solutions led first to his appointment on July 1, 1935, as Acting State Director of Rural Rehabilitation and Resettlement in Texas under the U.S. Resettlement Administration. He was offered the post by Dr. Carl C. Taylor, the Resettlement Administration Assistant Administrator for Rural Resettlement, whom he had known well for 10-15 years.

In Texas:

> Miserable cotton prices and drought spelled disaster for thousands.... For tenants, especially, there was no choice, as thousands were forced from the land by crop reduction programs. Indeed, from 1930 to 1940 sharecroppers and tenants declined by almost 60 percent...
> Rural Texans, once the embodiment of self-reliance, went on relief in huge numbers, providing 50 percent of the cases. Moreover, in turn, over 80 percent of these were farm laborers and tenants (Patenaude 1980, pp. 90, 98).

Rural rehabilitation was an attempt to help struggling farmers regain their independence via small loans accompanied by technical agricultural guidance. Wiley served as Acting Director through September 19, 1935, resigning to take a newly-created position in the Resettlement Administration headquarters office (Montgomery, Alabama) for the Southeast region. His appointment in Texas had been considered temporary, intended for one or two months, and almost from the start plans were underway in Washington, DC, and the Southeast regional office to promote and transfer him there as Regional Chief of Land Use Planning.

XII. LAND USE READJUSTMENTS IN THE SOUTHEAST

Wiley and his family left Texas for nearly a year when he assumed new duties beginning September 30, 1935 as Chief, Land Use Planning Section, U.S. Resettlement Administration, for Region V (Alabama, Georgia, South Carolina, and Florida) officed in Montgomery, Alabama. The Land Use Planning Section was part of the Division of Land Utilization.

The Cotton Belt of the Southeast contained some of the nation's most difficult problem areas during the Depression, and in the words of Rupert Vance published in 1936:

> ...areas of Georgia, South Carolina, and Alabama are the core of our problem zone. Not only does this section display the highest proportion of eroded soil, the densest pattern of tenancy, and the lowest standards of living, but it suffered the greatest weevil damage and has been the slowest region in recovering (Reed and Singal 1982, p. 105).

Richard T. Ely for many years had advocated the retirement of submarginal land. To Wiley the Resettlement Administration program presented the opportunity for:

> ...long-range planning that involved readjustments in land use, more economical sized farms, better systems of farming, feasible cooperative arrangements among farmers, soil conservation, retirement from use of submarginal crop lands, and opportunity for the resettling on good farm lands of farm families stranded on poor land (Wiley 1937c, p. 457).

As Regional Chief of Land Use Planning, Wiley became responsible to organize and administer the land use planning work of 5-15 technical personnel in the regional office and four state land planning specialists stationed in the four states. This work included making judgments on all land to be purchased or leased in the rural rehabilitation work and on project locations for land development and resettlement. It also included technical assistance on land inventory, land classification, land policies, and area program work in each of the four states.

The May 1936 issue of the *Journal of Farm Economics* carried a news item announcing that Wiley would be one of four regional land policy advisers assisting Wehrwein in conduct of a seminar on land use policy and problems at Iowa State College during the summer. The seminar would be attended by Resettlement Administration land use specialists from the north and south central states (Wehrwein 1936).

When Wiley left the University of Texas in September 1935 on a one-year leave of absence, there was some uncertainty in the economics department whether he would return. However, before the end of July 1936, he communicated his intent to return to his teaching position. Wiley served with the Resettlement Administration until he resumed teaching at Austin in September. His resignation from the Resettlement Administration was effective September 15, 1936.

At the time Wiley completed his one-year's service as Chief of the Land Use Planning Section in Region V, extensive land classification and related studies had been initiated in each of the four states:

> Although all the States of Region V are following a general program outlined by the regional office—reconnaissance land classification mapping, area programs of land use, and selection of resettlement areas—each State in turn is also following a program which considers its own particular problems.
>
> In *Alabama* under the direction of former Land-Use Planning Specialist Luther B. Fuller, Auburn, land ownership maps have been completed for 56 out of the 67 counties of the State, and it is anticipated that the work on the project will be completed soon.
>
> In *Florida*, Louis T. Nieland, Land-Use Planning Specialist (Municipal Building, Gainesville) is at work on a variety of projects. Land classification work in most of the counties is progressing, and maps are being made; a standard of living study has been made in Alachna county, and related to conditions of land-use; a special study on the adaptability of certain lands in Calhoun, Jackson, and Liberty counties for the growing of Chinese tung oil trees has been completed, as well as a special study on the Sugar Bowl Drainage District in Sarasota County.
>
> In *Georgia* a rather general land utilization report has been prepared, containing discussions on agriculture, manufacturing, mining, recreation, etc. A report has also been made on areas adapted to closer

settlement, and a detailed study of the Northeast Georgia Upland Game Conservation Project and the Georgia Coastal Flatwoods Upland Game Project has been made preliminary to land classification studies. Beauregard A. Russell, College of Agriculture, Athens, is Land-Use Planning Specialist in charge of these studies.

In *South Carolina*, land classification work is progressing, and in addition studies on the character and intent of ownership of all lands in the State by counties are in progress. W. B. Rogers of Clemson College, is State Land-Use Planning Specialist... (*Land Policy Circular* 1936, pp. 15-16).

Substantial land use readjustments were achieved in the Southeast. Some comparisons between Southeast and U.S. trends in acreage of principal crops harvested, from 1930 to 1955, will illustrate (Wooten and Anderson 1957, p. 43). In the 1930s the Southeast averaged 24 million acres yearly in principal crops harvested, and the United States averaged 334 million. During the period 1940-44, the Southeast average fell to 22 million acres while the U.S. average rose to 341 million. From 1945 to 1949, the Southeast average fell again to 18 million acres, while the U.S. average rose to 347 million. By 1955 the Southeast had less than 16 million acres in principal crops harvested, or approximately one-third below its 1930-39 average. The U.S. total stood at 333 million in 1955, or essentially identical with the national average in the 1930s.

Shifts of poor cropland to pasture and forest in the Southeast, a primary objective of the Resettlement Administration, had been achieved. These land use shifts, together with the significant outmigration, industrialization, and restructuring of the rural economy that accelerated during and after World War II, eventually brought rural levels of living in the Southeast much closer to desired standards.

Paul E. Mertz, in his book *New Deal Policy and Southern Rural Poverty*, observes that by the late 1930s there was a nascent realization that land in the South (previously regarded as the region's most valuable asset) "could not support all those dependent on it" (Mertz 1978, p. 233). Mertz quotes from a letter written by Clarence Roberts, editor of the *Oklahoma Farmer-Stockman*, to Will Alexander of the Farm Security Administra-

tion in January 1940. Roberts saw outmigration from the South
as the principal readjustment of people to land in years ahead:

> [Roberts] concluded that 'the nation as a whole must prepare to take
> care of the surplus population of the South,' because the region's
> 'resources...simply will not maintain the present population.'
> Furthermore, he wrote: 'The real situation is understood by only a
> few...in the field of agriculture who have the facts and are willing to
> look at them. The general public does not suspect the facts nor their
> significance. It does not suspect that it has already assumed the burden
> of support of a part of the South's rural population....They must get
> ready to support an even larger number in the immediate years ahead
> (Mertz 1978, pp. 251-252).

I believe that Wiley was one of the few who understood the
real situation.

XII. LATER SCHOLARSHIP:
EXAMINING THE INTEGRATED
ECONOMY AS SOLUTION

Wiley was willing to go along with rural rehabilitation as an
emergency measure, of temporary duration at a time when farm
families had almost no off-farm employment opportunities. But
when rural rehabilitation began to dominate Resettlement
Administration policies and programs, and took on the
character of a permanent solution to rural poverty, I believe he
saw in this the weakness and danger of agrarianism and
concluded he wanted no part in it. I feel this destroyed any
thoughts he may have had of staying in the Federal service.

Positions of higher responsibility in government apparently
were available to Alton Wiley. L. C. Gray, for instance, had
expressed a desire to bring Wiley into the Washington, DC
office of the Division of Land Utilization "for land use
planning work in a major position" (Wiecking 1935). Back
in Texas Wiley was urged to run for public office (Wiley, Joe
M., 1992-93).

However, Wiley had developed an aversion to government
employment:

Dad hated regimentation and was disgusted with government bureaucrats that he met when working in Rural Rehab and Land Use Planning. In spite of this he would argue for government control or orchestration of economic factors in both agriculture and industry in order to avoid wide swings in the cycles. Years ago I felt this to be too inconsistent; now I don't see a better alternative (Wiley, Gerald A., 1992).

Furthermore, Evans recalls Wiley's feeling that "for an economist to voice what public opinion decreed was to become only a political henchman" (Evans n.d., p. 6). Wiley preferred the relative freedom to speak his mind as a university professor and occasional consultant to the Federal government.

As seen earlier in the Duval dissertation, Wiley's concern for integration of the specialized exchange economy was passed along to and through his students. Another indication comes from the 1937 master's thesis by Malvin Montgomery, "The Agricultural Adjustment Administration and the Cotton Farmer," which Wiley supervised:

The division of labor, typical of industrial society, has given us the efficiency enabling a relatively few farmers to feed the nation while most of the laborers have been free to apply the new industrial techniques in the making of the great variety of goods composing our standard of living...But we have become so engrossed in the incidentals of engaging in successful business enterprise that we have come to underemphasize the fundamentals of division of labor—that each unit or industry must integrate its activities with those of all the others...The farmer is one very important link in a chain of production. Without him the process is helpless, just as it is without any one of the other important links: transportation, communication, exchange, manufacturing, mining, etc. In an industrial society agriculture is just as important as any other primary unit—no more (Montgomery 1937, pp. iii-iv).

However, in the depth of the depression of the 1930s, agriculture took on greater importance to national economic recovery. Cotton was possibly the most important agricultural commodity in relation to the total U.S. economy. Cotton was the leading cash crop in the United States, and in the international exchange economy U.S. cotton exports provided the basis for a high proportion of imports of manufactured goods from other countries. An entire region...the Cotton Belt of the South...was dependent on the cotton economy. When the cotton economy went down, the purchasing power of the South and its contribution to the U.S. economy went down too. Moreover, when cotton profits and production fell, a large share of U.S. purchasing power in the international exchange economy fell with it. Montgomery's thesis defended the New Deal cotton program primarily on the strength of what it achieved by redistributing national income and restoring purchasing power to cotton farmers and the southern population generally, whose long pent-up demand for goods and services implied a high marginal propensity to consume and resulting stimulus to national economic recovery.

Wiley's concern for the integrated economy was heightened by observing the forces of disintegration associated with the Depression. According to Odum and Moore, whose research was published in 1938:

> ...when the demands and sweep of artificial society and of supertechnological processes exceed the natural capacity of the people or of a living culture to absorb and adjust, and when there are inadequate media of integration and leadership, there must inevitably be crisis, maladjustment; and if the process goes on long enough, disintegration...How much could the people stand? How much would their institutions bear? How much ahead of the people were the thought, ideologies, and technologies of the leaders? If there was not a natural capacity for adjustment, on the one hand, or a directed guidance, on the other, survival was not likely. Here were new dilemmas of artificial society and supertechnology which the nation had not yet faced....The scene of the New Deal, therefore, reflected a dramatic crisis which demanded heroic men and measures without which must come greater chaos (Odum and Moore 1938, p. 629).

Odum and Moore viewed integration from the standpoint of regionalism and regional integration into the national economy and life. Regionalism was applied functionalism, whereby human society is seen as a differentiated whole consisting of interdependent parts and the function of each part is described and considered for its contribution to the whole. Integration implies a means of collaboration between the parts. In another book Odum linked integration with *balance*, saying "region-alism itself is primarily interested in the total integration and balance of these regions" so that the regions "may be more adequate in all aspects of resources and culture" (Odum 1951, p. 358).

XIII. WARTIME EMPHASES

Throughout his career, Wiley had been an occasional speaker at high schools (including commencements), meetings of businessmens' groups and farm organizations, and so forth. During World War II Wiley became a frequent speaker at forums of students, civic groups, and military personnel, on topics ranging from the wartime food problem and postwar planning, to democracy and the politics of labor and provisions of the Bretton Woods international monetary conference of 1944. Newspaper accounts indicate that he addressed agricultural issues such as:

> How much of the food problem is not one of actual production, but of distribution? What is the consumer's, including the university student's, responsibility in the food crisis? Shall we feed the post-war hungry peoples of the world? Is there a possibility of a back-to-the-farm movement after the war? Can we avoid stagnation in our economy?

Asked whether the farmers, the people, or the bureaucrats should plan the war food policy, Wiley said:

> It is the technical economist's job. It takes more than a knowledge of raising beans, pears, and pork, more than a consumer's interest to do it. Congress will have to o.k. the plan, but they will have to take the advice of technicians (*The Daily Texan*, 1943).

XIV.   POSTWAR AGRICULTURAL ADJUSTMENT AND POLICY

Wiley's views on postwar agricultural adjustment and policy are revealed in his address to the Tenth Cotton Research Congress (held July 1949 in Dallas), where he offered a program of adjustment for the cotton economy. His paper was titled "Cotton in an Agricultural Program," and his proposed adjustments included the need for many cotton farmers to find other occupations.

In his address to the Cotton Research Congress, Wiley indicated that the cotton program should be designed "on the basis of adjustments dictated by efficiency." It should be designed to "save agriculture and the cotton economy and to promote a more complete integration of these with the total economy..." (Wiley 1949, p. 48). But Wiley made clear that by saving agriculture he did not mean saving farmers, and by saving the cotton economy he did not mean saving cotton farmers:

> If we cherish efficiency and productivity, it is imperative that we distinguish *saving farmers* and *saving agriculture*, and likewise distinguish programs for *cotton farmers* and programs for *the cotton economy*—cotton producers and allied industries inclusive. Of course, in view of technologically dictated adjustments in both production and processing patterns, that is with the presence of cheap, competitive fibers, the magnitude of the total cotton economy would have to shrink proportionally thereto. But to 'lose weight' is not necessarily contrary to the objective of 'good health.' That illustrates what I mean by saying that it may be necessary to sacrifice some cotton farmers in order to save the cotton economy (Wiley 1948, p. 49).

As a longtime observer and analyst of farm price and income support programs, Wiley stated his guidelines for price support programs. His general guidelines are of particular interest:

> Rationally, the character of price supports should be so framed as to facilitate the achievement of program objectives, rather than work independently of, or contrariwise to, those ends. I have a feeling since the beginning of our price support programs that they have been framed, too frequently, independently of long-run goals, or if not that, as if long-run objectives were not basic to intelligent planning of price support programs. And I do not intend this observation to be interpreted to mean that I am an opponent of price supports in all forms. I do believe, however, that we should know what our price support programs are to achieve in the way of needed economic adjustments, and have some standard of measurement whereby we may measure results achieved....

I am of the opinion that a price support program to save our cotton economy must stem from the fact that surpluses and relatively low prices are associated with one or the other of three types of price relationships; namely, 1) the chronic, or long-run, situation, 2) the cyclical depression phase, and 3) seasonal situations. Uniform price support programs should not apply to each of these situations, for the reason that uniformity of application of price supports to each of these phases of the problem gets variable results, some of which run counter, rather than supplementary to, program objectives (Wiley 1948, pp. 52-53).

Wiley basically felt that price supports should be used only during short-run emergencies:

In reference to the need for support programs, are we not justified in the assumption that the occasion for price supports—on some sort of parity basis—has foundations in the existence of surpluses, relatively low prices—especially relative to costs; and that these resolve themselves ultimately into sufficient market outlets at prices satisfactory, at least, to many producers?

....So to subsidize surplus farmers to remain in—and possibly to expand—cotton production would only add maladjustment to maladjustment.

...price support programs need be applied only when more or less short-run situations unbalance production and market outlet relationships (Wiley 1948, p. 53).

In 1950 Wiley was named a technical adviser on agricultural economics to the Committee on the Southwest Economy appointed by Leon Keyserling, chairman of President Truman's Council of Economic Advisers. The committee, of which Ayres was a member, was charged to examine opportunities for economic development, identify obstacles, and analyze potentials for long-term development to guide public and private action. The committee's report was completed in 1954.

XV.   IN DEFENSE OF ACADEMIC FREEDOM

On November 1, 1944, University of Texas President Homer P. Rainey was fired by the Regents in a continuing battle over academic freedom. In the 1930s and 40s Rainey had defended several University of Texas professors, including Wiley, whose progressive views drew the ire of certain ultra-conservative leaders in the state.

Professors Wiley, Hale, Montgomery, and Ayres had New Deal connections, Hale also was understood to be teaching Marxism, and the whole place was just too "radical" to suit the demagogues. Near the end of 1940 the conflict became intense, and one or more members of the university's Regents tried to force Rainey to dismiss the four economics professors, which he wouldn't do.

When Ronnie Dugger was writing his fine book on the University of Texas, he interviewed Montgomery. Dugger asked why Wiley, the least controversial of the four, had been a target, and Montgomery is quoted as replying: "Oh, Wiley was intelligent—but *right-wing!*" (Dugger 1974, p. 419). Lest anyone think that Wiley was reactionary or even conservative, Montgomery's statement needs clarification.

Montgomery, who was known as a comic and often made patently absurd statements for effect, was facetious in referring to Alton Wiley as right-wing. Had Wiley been right-wing, the ultra-conservatives surely would not have sought his dismissal.

Early in 1941 a committee of the Texas Senate drafted a bill that was not acted upon but would have provided for immediate dismissal of any schoolteacher or professor whose teachings were "inimical" to the Constitution. According to George Norris Green:

> Economics professor C. A. Wiley testified at one of the few committee meetings open to the public that there was no certainty of what 'inimical' meant. It might be construed to include the criticism of some part of the Constitution as obsolete or the proposal of an amendment (Green 1979, p. 73).

At the time Rainey was fired, Wiley clearly was understood to be a liberal. Roy Bedichek, Director of the Bureau of Public School Service, University of Texas, during that era of controversy over academic freedom, wrote in a letter to a friend in 1944:

The University has grown very rich, and the rich love it like a brother. They don't want to see it prostituted by fellows like Montgomery, Ayres, Wiley, Hale, or any defender of theirs. Rainey happened to come along believing in academic freedom and with a will to defend that freedom. That's the nub of the whole controversy. The Regents call it lack of cooperation on the part of Rainey; Rainey calls it an attempt to purge the liberal elements from the Faculty....But I am greatly concerned over the outcome of the big fight, which is going to determine whether Texas youth are going to be taught in the future by intellectual geldings, or permitted contact with what Whitman calls the great seminal ideas of our time. The fight looks rather hopeless at present (Bedichek 1985, pp. 247, 249).

Wiley's son Gerald states:

> ...he was liberal and a democrat. He thought F. D. Roosevelt could do no wrong, and someone told me Dad was active in the conventions leading to F.D.R.'s nomination for President (Wiley, Gerald A. 1992).

His brother Joe says, though their father "might have been considered a liberal or middle-of-the-roader, he certainly was not a radical" (Wiley, Joe M. 1992-93).

Others who later knew Wiley consider him a liberal and differ only on the degree of his liberalism. Evans contends that "Clarence Wiley was as liberal as were the other Texas Institutionalists of that era" (Evans n.d. p. 2). McDonald, however, feels Wiley was more moderate:

> ...Wiley was a liberal Democrat (and a true democrat, lower-case d), but one who was more moderate than the others under attack. I would not characterize him as 'left-wing' in an unqualified sense; and I certainly would not characterize him as 'right-wing' in *any* meaningful sense (McDonald 1992b).

University of Texas economics professors pursued the spirit of free inquiry, according to James H. Street, "with great personal courage in an atmosphere of severe intimidation and constant threat of a loss of livelihood if they spoke out in a manner that the members of the State Legislature, who controlled the University budget, considered revolutionary or

subversive of the young" (Street n.d., pp. 3-4). Wiley continued
to publicly speak his mind when necessary. An immediate
instance came in 1945, when Wiley defended President
Roosevelt's controversial appointment in March of former Vice
President and Secretary of Agriculture Henry A. Wallace as
Secretary of Commerce, to replace Texan Jesse Holman Jones
who had held the post since 1940. Countering charges that the
appointment was a political move and that Wallace was not
qualified for this cabinet position, Wiley publicly supported the
appointment and said Wallace was "fully capable of handling
the position" (*The Daily Texan*, 1945).

XVI.   WILEY'S LEGACY FOR
THE 1990s AND BEYOND

Wiley suffered two cerebral hemorrhages in the spring of 1956
and died in a San Antonio hospital on April 27, 1956; he is
buried in Johnson City. He was divorced from his first wife and
in 1955 had married Mrs. Mary Dean Drinkard of Austin. He
was survived by his widow, three children, three sisters (Maggie,
Nettie, and Laura), and two brothers (Ollie and Horace).

Clarence Alton Wiley skillfully applied his institutionalist
insights toward the solving of society's problems, while often
using orthodox tools of economic analysis. Possibly Wiley's
greatest contribution to societal problem-solving in his lifetime
was to advance the realization that the performance of the
American rural economy now is determined by performance of
the integrated aggregate economy and that agriculture and rural
people need to be better integrated into the aggregate economy.
Wiley's insistence on this realization, with all its implications
for maladjustments and readjustments of natural, human,
capital, and entrepreneurial resources, contributed to the
reshaping of U.S. agricultural and rural development policy.

Consequently, and of lasting importance, Wiley's concept of
rural America in an integrated economy provides a unique
organizing view for work toward solving problems of rural
America in the 1990s and beyond. While U.S. population, land

uses, and economic activities are distributed differently than when Wiley was alive and many other conditions also have changed, the basic problems of rural America remain the same. Wiley sets the integrated economy as the desirable end-state toward which worldwide economic activity is tending in the interest of efficiency. Therefore, the test of any private or public economic decision affecting rural America becomes: *How does it contribute to fuller integration of the rural economy within the aggregate economy?* Those rural areas that succeed in more fully integrating will prosper; those that don't will not.

ACKNOWLEDGMENTS

I am greatly indebted to Stephen L. McDonald, Ralph L. Elder, Jean Richardson, and Ronnie J. Phillips for assistance in researching and writing this chapter.

Chapter 7

Erich W. Zimmermann,
The Dynamics of Resourceship

Stephen L. McDonald

"Resources *are* not, they *become*; they are not static but expand and contract in response to human wants and human actions."

EWZ (1951) p. 18.

"Knowledge is truly the mother of all other resources."

EWZ (1951) p. 10.

I. INTRODUCTION

The ideas expressed in the above quotations epitomize the profoundly original and richly lasting contributions of Erich W. Zimmermann to the discipline of economics—contributions that radiate far beyond the subject of natural resources and their uses. These ideas originated in his thought many years before he came to the University of Texas, but it was there that they came to fullest fruition and influenced the greatest number of his graduate students.

As one of those students in the years (1947-1950) when he was most actively revising and expanding the first edition (1933) of his monumental *World Resources and Industries* and expounding his still developing ideas in the classroom, I contend that he was an integral member of the group identified in the present volume as the "Texas School" of economics. He influenced and was influenced by the teachings of the other major members discussed here. His frame of reference—his socio-economic approach—was essentially the same as theirs. His emphasis on technology as the dynamic element, and on institutions as the conservative element, in the evolution of economies and societies both complemented and reinforced that of his colleagues. So, too, his rejection of the "harmonic" view of the workings of the price system and his willingness to accept a large role for government as regulator and active contributor to stability.[1]

That Zimmermann seemed immune to the outside attacks suffered by some of the others of the "Texas School" is due, I think, partly to his original, and later joint, appointment in the College of Business Administration, but chiefly to his more reserved way of expressing the implications of his teachings. He was not a policy activist. He never came across to the outside community as a "dangerous radical." Indeed, as we shall see, the only thing really endangered by his work was the static view of natural resources.

I believe that the following exposition and evaluation of Zimmermann's mature thought, based chiefly on its final statement in the 1951 edition of *World Resources and Industries,* will support my contention that he was a full member of the "Texas School" but, much more importantly, will demonstrate that his original ideas and approach are a fundamental and permanent contribution to the larger discipline of economics. His explanation of the dynamics of resourceship (the quality of being a resource), with technological progress playing the active role, is today even more relevant to the problems of economic development and the management of depletable (or degradable) resources than in his time. But first, a brief biographical sketch to throw some light on the stages of his intellectual growth.

II. ZIMMERMANN'S LIFE
AND PRINCIPAL WORKS

Erich Walter Zimmermann was born in Mainz, Germany, on July 31, 1888, the son of Wilhelm and Eugenie (Gruneberg) Zimmermann.[2] (On several occasions that I recall, but in what contexts I forget, Zimmermann stated that his father was a "Prussian bureaucrat." He may have been trying to convey something other than region of origin.) Following graduation from gymnasium at Dusseldorf in 1907, he studied at the universities of Berlin, Munich, Birmingham (England) and Bonn, taking the Ph.D. degree at the last-named in 1911. His dissertation, based largely on materials gathered personally "in the field" in England, Scotland and Wales, was entitled *Die britische Kohlenausfuhr, ihre Geschicte, Organisation und Bedeutung*, which may be translated as *The British Coal Export Trade: Its History, Organization and Significance.*

While Zimmermann was studying at Bonn, the leading economic theorist there was Heinrich Dietzel, who accepted the neoclassical framework but retained some of the influence of his own teacher, Adolf Wagner, who had taken the broader "social economy" approach. The professors under whom Zimmermann studied at Berlin, Munich and Birmingham, and who undoubtedly influenced his thinking also, are not known. In any case, as has already been seen, Zimmermann's mature approach, while a blend, owes more to the socio-economic than to the neoclassical.

Immediately upon taking the Ph.D. degree, Zimmermann came to the United States to do research on the role of the Great Lakes in the pattern of North American transportation. He supported himself initially by teaching at a Kentucky mountain school and later at a New York City preparatory school. It is not clear whether he came to the United States intending to return to Germany upon completion of his research. In any case, he was destined to stay. No doubt the outbreak of war in Europe in 1914 was a factor. From 1915 to 1918, Zimmermann served as an instructor of economics and sociology at New York University. At some point the Great Lakes project was

abandoned, but the material he had gathered may have
contributed to the book he co-authored with W. C. Clark,
Foreign Trade and Shipping, published in 1917 (Zimmermann
and Clark 1917). Also in 1917, on June 23, he married Margaret
Hoff. They were to have three children: Ericka Sophia, Charles
Hoff and Margaret Eugenia.

In 1918 Zimmermann accepted an associate professorship of
commerce at James Milliken University in Decatur, Illinois.
The first year was probably a trial year, since he was promoted
to the rank of professor in the following year. While there he
published another book, *Zimmermann on Ocean Shipping*
(Zimmermann 1921). More significantly, perhaps, it was at
James Millikin that he began to teach a course entitled
"Resources and Industries." No doubt the book that was in 1933
to make his reputation as "the outstanding authority in this
country on natural resources..."[3] was germinated there in the
early 'twenties. His growing interest in natural resources was
surely stimulated by, and probably reflected in, his service as
consulting economist to the Bureau of Mines, U. S. Department
of the Interior, from 1920 to 1923.

Zimmermann's next move was to the University of North
Carolina in 1922, where he taught for twenty years. He started
with an associate professorship, but was promoted to the rank
of professor of economics in 1925. While working assiduously
on the great book to come, he served as a member of The
Brookings Institution research staff on Puerto Rico in 1929,
contributing to the final report, *Porto Rico and Its Problems*
(Zimmermann et al., 1930) traveled in Europe gathering
material under a grant from the Social Science Research
Council, and lectured under various auspices in Kiel, Berlin
and Mannheim.

When *World Resources and Industries* appeared in 1933
(Zimmermann 1933a) it was greeted with critical acclaim.
Widely reviewed in major journals, it was consistently
praised for its originality, comprehensiveness and clarity.
A typical comment was that of Walter C. Langsam of
Columbia University:

Unusual and novel in its method of studying world resources, Professor Zimmermann's work stands out as a pioneer effort in the field of cultural economics. It is, perhaps, not too much to say that no one may regard himself as well-informed in the spheres of economics, geography or history unless he becomes acquainted with this epoch-making study (Langsam 1934, pp. 457-459).

In 1934 Zimmermann was presented the Mayflower Society Cup award for his rare accomplishment and became holder of the distinguished professorship at North Carolina named the Kenan Professorship. His fame led to numerous invitations to lecture at universities in Europe and the United States, including the University of Texas in 1941. From 1936 to 1939, he was a member of the Institute for International Cooperation's American coordinating committee for international studies; and in 1939-1940 was Director of Research to President Roosevelt's Interdepartmental Committee on Puerto Rico.

Following Zimmermann's lecture at Texas in 1941, it was decided by the faculty and relevant administrators to offer him a distinguished professorship in resources in the College of Business Administration. The offer was delayed one year because one of the regents, who were then required by state law to give unanimous consent to an offer of a distinguished professorship, raised an objection of an undisclosed nature. Probably it had to do with a question about Zimmermann's sentiments regarding his native country's aggressions in Europe since 1939, for the appointment was approved in 1942 after President Homer P. Rainey assured the regents in writing that there could be no question of Zimmermann's total loyalty to the United States.[4] (He had become a naturalized citizen sixteen years before, in 1925.) Toward the end of World War II, he was asked by the Secretary of the Navy to participate in a conference on Foundations of National Power. He was later to teach a popular course at the University of Texas on the same subject.

After the War, Zimmermann received many other invitations in recognition of his distinction. He served as visiting professor at the University of California and at Columbia University. He became a director of the National Bureau of Economic Research and a member of the Advisory Committee for American Participation in the International Congress for Conservation of Natural Resources of the United Nations. He was asked to sit on the President's Council of Economic Advisors but declined due to poor health.

Meanwhile, graduate students in economics were increasingly attracted to his courses, and both Zimmermann and the faculty of the economics department desired a more formal association. So in 1947 he was reappointed jointly in the Department of Economics (College of Arts and Sciences) and the College of Business Administration, and awarded a distinguished professorship in economics in addition to the one he already held in the latter college. He thus became the only faculty member of the University of Texas to hold a double distinguished professorship. It is significant that thereafter in identifying his rank he listed his professorship in economics before the one in resources, even though the latter was first in time; and he was highly sensitive to any student failure to recognize his second distinction. Another distinction came in 1949 in the form of an honorary degree, Doctor of Laws, awarded by Washington and Lee University. (Perhaps in fun—one could not always tell—he once told his class that in Germany he would be addressed as Herr Doctor Doctor Professor Professor.)

The revised version of *World Resources and Industries* (hereinafter *WRI*) came out in 1951 and was even more highly acclaimed than the first. As one reviewer said, "When Zimmermann's first edition of *World Resources and Industries* appeared in 1933 it was highly praised by all reviewers: the new edition is superior in every way." (Walter 1952-53, pp. 59-60) Those of us who had sat in his classes in the preceding few years, using the 1933 edition as a text, had had a preview in the form of his lucid lectures. We knew what new material would be in the revised one. But even among those who had since taken their degrees, many to my knowledge rushed to buy a copy of the revised edition to treasure and consult for the rest of their lives. This is written with my copy, so acquired, before me.

Zimmermann's final major work was *Conservation in the Production of Petroleum: A Study in Industrial Control,* published in 1957 (Zimmermann 1957a). This too is a learned, thoughtful and thoroughly researched book, to be valued highly if for no more than its lucid explanation of the basic issue involved and its detailed account of the process by which that issue had been handled in the United States as a matter of practical policy.

Erich W. Zimmermann died February 16, 1961, and is buried in Austin, Texas. But his famed textbook could not be allowed to expire with him. Three years after his death, the first 10 chapters were published as a separate volume entitled *Introduction to World Resources* (Zimmermann 1964). In 1972, a third edition of the whole work was published as *Zimmermann's World Resources and Industries,* as revised by W. N. Peach and James A. Constantin (Peach and Constantin 1972). Two posthumous honors illustrate the regard in which his contributions are still held at the University of Texas: the creation in 1984 of the Erich W. Zimmermann Regents Professorship in Geography, and his induction in 1985 into the College of Business Administration's Hall of Fame.

III. ZIMMERMANN'S DYNAMIC THEORY OF RESOURCESHIP

Zimmermann defined "resource" in a functional way. As he put it,

> The word "resource" *does not refer to a thing or a substance but to a function which a thing or substance may perform or to an operation in which it may take part,* namely, the function or operation of attaining a given end such as satisfying a want. In other words, the word 'resource' is an abstraction reflecting human appraisal and relating to a function or operation. (Emphasis in original.) (Zimmermann, 1951 p. 7).

Thus he saw natural resources not simply as things that occur in nature but as those aspects of the natural environment that human beings have been able and have chosen to utilize in satisfying their wants. The importance of a resource lies not in the physical quantity of it in nature, but in the magnitude of the wants societies may satisfy through its utilization.

If we abstract from human beings and their cultures, the substances and processes occurring in the crust of the earth and its atmosphere are, in Zimmermann's words, merely "neutral stuff."[5] But when human beings and their cultures impact on these substances and processes, *some parts* of them are converted into either resources or anti-resources, the latter of which Zimmermann labeled "resistances," since they hinder the satisfaction of wants in various ways. The other parts remain neutral, awaiting cultural change and additional conversion of them into either resources or resistances. Thus the effective (net) quantity and variety of natural resources is culturally relative. And so are wants; they too are altered by cultural change.

So the key to resourceship, given the "stuff" of the earth and its atmosphere, is culture. Zimmermann sees "culture," in its turn, as divisible into two sets of "arts," the technological arts and the societal arts, the latter closely associated with institutions. The former, resting upon scientific knowledge, define the technical abilities of a culture to produce want-satisfying goods and services by efficiently combining human and other resources. The latter, resting less upon science and more upon long custom, faith, ideals and historical power relationships, define the ways in which human beings are expected to behave in relation to each other and the physical environment and thus affect their abilities to organize themselves and cooperate in the production of goods and services. These two aspects of culture interact with each other and with nature to create and destroy resources.

Technological advance enables societies not only to utilize additional natural substances and processes, the new often substituting for the old, but also to overcome resistances and to increase the want-satisfying capacity of a given physical quantity of a substance. Consider the case of petroleum. Its "creation" as an energy resource was obviously associated with the perfection of the internal combustion engine, a major advance over its precursor, the steam engine. Petroleum substantially displaced coal as a source of energy, especially in mobile applications, and it helped overcome the "resistance" of distance between concentrations of economic activity. It freed land for the production of human foods by allowing the substitution of the tractor for draft animals. Enlargement of the fraction of it convertible to gasoline, and improvements in the conversion of gasoline into power and distance traveled, have effectively—that is, functionally—increased the size of the world's petroleum resources. And once it was created, the physical quantities of this resource available for use have been maintained and expanded thus far by advances in the technology of discovery and extraction. Although technological advance has destructive aspects also, its dominant thrust is creative.

The societal arts, on the other hand, may be either creative of resources or inhibitory. Social institutions that reward intellectual creativity, allow free entry and promote competition, facilitate adjustments by those suffering damage from technological innovation rather than protect them in the *status quo ante*—such institutions, by removing barriers to the application of new technology, are effectively creative of new and enlarged resources. But rapid technological change tends to demand rapid institutional change, and social institutions are in their nature resistant to change. After all, they exist to provide some certainty in human relations—some predictability of human behavior—because of the constraints on behavior they impose by law, custom and belief.[6] No person can afford to enter into long-term commitments if the law, for instance, is subject to rapid and unpredictable changes.

But there is a more fundamental barrier to rapid institutional innovation identified by Zimmermann. It has to do with the difference between knowledge and belief. The knowledge underlying technology is verifiable through experiment and demonstration. Beliefs underlying social institutions are not. Consequently, there cannot be different systems of scientific knowledge in different cultures; but there can be and are many different systems of beliefs and institutions, and the latter can be more or less inhibitory of technological innovation. Technology has the potential to change rapidly because the underlying advances in knowledge are verifiable as advances. Institutions are more resistant to change because the beliefs underlying proposals of change are not so verifiable as advances. The result is a "lopsided development of the arts." (Zimmermann 1951, p. 38).

Here we have a distinct echo of the dominant thesis of Veblen, Ayres and Dewey, which every institutionalist will recognize. Technological advance is the dynamic element in the growth and development of societies, while institutions are at best passive and at worst inhibitory. The reason for the difference is the differential verifiability of the knowledge that underlies technology, the superiority, as Ayres chose to put it, of "instrumental valuation" over reliance on faith, custom and authority.[7]

In any case, we can see now why Zimmermann would characteristically say that "knowledge is truly the mother of all other resources," why he viewed resources as being more or less continuously created and destroyed by technological advance despite lagging adjustment of the "societal arts." The destruction side of the dynamics is not a matter of exhaustion— of "running out"—but rather of replacement to some degree with something superior. The implications of such a view of natural resources are even more astonishing today, in a world perennially worried about physical limits and the supposedly dire need to conserve our "diminishing" resources, than when Zimmermann was writing them down. He is saying to us still that the only true limit is man's knowledge and his ingenuity in applying it.

One other insight of Zimmermann's before we turn to some of the applications of his dynamic theory of resourceship. Zimmermann believed that the real key to man's increasing powers of production is *energy*.[8] He held that what we call the "industrial revolution" was not just a mechanical revolution— not simply a revolution in the amount of real capital per worker—but rather an *energy* revolution, more specifically a revolution in the amount of *inanimate* energy employed per worker. Mechanical devices have been used by man for millenia. But until the eighteenth century, the only significant sources of inanimate energy employed were diffused sunlight, wood, wind and flowing water, all renewable in nature if not prevented by man. The industrial revolution opened up and rested upon a vast new class of inanimate energy sources: concentrated and stored solar energy in the forms of coal, petroleum and natural gas. These and the metal materials from which the new machines were chiefly made are, of course, nonrenewable. Thus it would appear to those still bound to the purely physical view of natural resources that the high living standards growing out of the industrial revolution are unsustainable in the long run, that disaster awaits us when the natural deposits of fossil fuels run out as they eventually "must." But if resources are essentially the creation of man and his "arts" in interaction with nature, as Zimmermann brilliantly argued, this pessimistic view of the future may be wholly unjustified. If the feared disaster occurs, it will not be due to the limitations of nature but to the limitations of man's knowledge and ingenuity, including his social ingenuity.

The natural nonrenewability of the resources of the modern industrial society raises the issue of conservation, and what it functionally means, to a new level. Conservation of something that can be physically exhausted is different from conservation of a process or material that is in nature renewable. We shall see how Zimmermann dealt with the conservation issue at a later point. It will help, first, to see how he applied his dynamic theory of resourceship to two great industries, agriculture and petroleum extraction.

IV.   THE RESOURCES OF AGRICULTURE AND THE "FARM PROBLEM"

Zimmermann taught three graduate courses in resources, using a different section of *World Resources and Industries* (1933 or 1951) as text in each. The first course, entitled "Introduction to Resources," covered the theory of resourceship as outlined above. The second was called "Resources of Agriculture," and the third "Resources of Industry." The latter two were in large measure descriptive (as to materials, technology and location) but they also provided "real world" illustrations of his dynamic theory. I shall concentrate on a couple of those illustrations.

Zimmermann saw agriculture much as Wiley did.[9] It is an industry dependent on naturally renewable processes and subject to the hazards of climate and the diseases and insect pests of plants and animals. When Zimmermann was writing, most of the world's agriculture remained unmechanized and dependent on animate energy. Its land units were therefore small by today's standards and often distant from centers of population, especially in the functional sense of time required per mile of travel. Farm households generally lacked electricity and the household appliances and communication devices available to urban residents. Their social interactions were different and less frequent than those of city dwellers. In short, the "way of life" was different, from the technology employed to the institutions. Zimmermann used the term "aloof" to describe the situation of agriculture in relation to the rest of the economy. Wiley described it as "unintegrated." An associated condition was the relative poverty of the farm population.

The output of agriculture can be summarized as food, feed and fiber. The income elasticity and the price elasticity of demand for these products are both low—well below unity. The former means that at a given real price, the demand for these products tends to grow more slowly than the real incomes of consumers. The latter means that the variability of crop size, due to the above unpredictable natural hazards, produces even greater variability in real prices received. Most farm costs are fixed costs, even the costs of labor, most of which is supplied by family members. Farmers therefore have little incentive to restrict output when they experience or anticipate lower real prices. The resulting instability of income makes it especially difficult for farmers to acquire credit on good terms and frequently results in the bankruptcy of those who do have access to credit.[10]

A key institution in American agriculture, especially, is the family farm. On such a farm, children can be an asset; and the population reproduction rate among agriculturists tends to be higher than among urban dwellers. Family members cannot be "laid off" like urban workers when their services are unprofitable to the head of the farm household, and their subsistence, at least, becomes a fixed cost as noted earlier. In addition, family members normally working in urban jobs but unemployed and without early prospects must be "taken in" if they return to the family household and farm. Thus the institution of the family farm contributes to the instability of farm income and the persistent low returns to labor in agriculture.

It also tends to slow the introduction of mechanized methods, particularly the substitution of the tractor (and inanimate energy) for draft animals. It does so partly through contributing to income instability and hence credit rationing. More fundamentally, it does so by contributing to a continuing pressure of labor upon land in an economy subject to episodes of large-scale unemployment in the urban sector. The full mechanization of agriculture requires steady net outmigration to allow the remaining farm population to block up the larger acreages required to make such mechanization economically feasible. As Zimmermann rightly observed, taking advantage of the technological possibilities in agriculture and thus raising the standard of living of farmers depends upon steady expansion of the *nonagricultural* sectors of the economy (Zimmermann 1951, p. 174).[11] Periodic bouts of unemployment and underutilized capacity in the nonagricultural sectors hamper the adjustments in the land-and-capital per worker required to raise the real incomes of farmers to parity with those in other occupations.

The truth of this proposition is vividly illustrated by contrasting the agricultural experience during the Depression with that following World War II, which among other things released a huge dammed-up and underemployed stock of labor for more productive uses. The result was an explosion of mechanization, restructuring of resource use, and elevated farm incomes. Now, American agriculture, at least, is no longer "aloof" or "unintegrated." Its integration is symbolized by the modern term "agri-business," by the farm home containing every appliance and device of communication and entertainment, by the framed college diploma hanging on the study wall, by the fifteen minute drive on a well-paved road to the nearest modern school (and its Friday night football game), supermarket, restaurant, theater and church. The family farm is still an organizational reality in America, but it is no longer a peculiar institution.

The modern industrial revolution in American agriculture also illustrates Zimmermann's creation and destruction of resources. Full mechanization did away with land uses previously required for the feeding and housing of draft animals, as well as cows, hogs and chickens kept to provide food for direct family consumption, and converted the freed land to the production of commercial products. It did away with the woodlot that previously supplied fuel and fenceposts and converted it also to commercial uses. It did away with the cultivation of rocky soils on highly erodable hillsides and converted old fields so situated to tree farms or pastures. It put a premium on large expanses of flat land more amenable to the use of heavy and expensive equipment and to irrigation. It enhanced the resourceship of minerals convertible to chemical fertilizers and insecticides. It weakened the "resistance" of distance and opened lands remote from population centers to intensive uses.

In short, technological advances in agriculture, including the development of improved plants and animals, have transformed the industry and freed labor resources for more productive uses, but not without the prior or simultaneous weakening of certain institutional impediments—the family farm as an institution to be sentimentally preserved, and a *laissez faire* attitude toward macroeconomic fluctuations.

V. THE RESOURCES OF INDUSTRY AND THE PROBLEM OF PETROLEUM CONSERVATION

As earlier indicated, Zimmermann attached special importance to inanimate energy; and to him the petroleum industry, in both its oil and gas aspects, epitomized modern society's heavy reliance on such energy. I shall accordingly concentrate on this industry to further illustrate his dynamic theory and his recognition of a major institutional impediment to the efficient use of the underlying natural materials.

Minerals in general belong to that class of "stuff" that occurs naturally in the earth's crust and is made available for human use through some form of "mining."[12] Although some types of mineral "stuffs" are recyclable to a degree, all are for practical purposes nonrenewable in nature, so that the term "mining" is often used as a synonym for "using up." This is especially true in the case of mineral fuels, which are inescapably converted in use to heat and gases generally too diffused to capture for further use. But as Zimmermann's dynamic theory makes clear, the quality of nonrenewability does not necessarily mean that we shall ever use up all of the natural materials in question. Nor does it necessarily mean an inevitable limit to advances in human welfare. The material "stuff" is not the *resource*, and new substitute *resources* can be created by man.

In the mineral extraction industries, a familiar concept is "reserves." Often the ratio of reserves to current production is used by the layman to imply the number of years' consumption we "have left." As Zimmermann explains, this use is incorrect and quite misleading. Reserves of a mineral are best interpreted as a working inventory. They are the *proven* quantities expected to be *profitably* recoverable from *known* deposits using *available* technology. While extraction from the inventory, considered alone, reduces the quantity remaining, concurrent exploration and development tend to replace what is withdrawn by increasing the number of known, prospectively profitable deposits. Technological progress tends both to increase the fraction of the "stuff" in known deposits it is profitable to recover[13] and to increase the probability and lower the cost of finding new deposits at greater depth or in less accessible places. If technological progress is insufficient to allow inventory replacement at constant real costs, then the relative prices of the mineral and its derivatives tend to rise, increasing the fraction of profitably recoverable "stuff" in known deposits, putting a premium on intensified R & D effort, and discouraging the consumption of the mineral in favor of substitutes in some uses.

Thus "inevitable running out" is a false specter. Premature, hence wasteful, abandonment for substitutes is the real issue.

Oil and gas are peculiarly subject to this kind of waste in a *laissez faire* institutional setting. Unlike hard-rock minerals, they are mobile underground and are extracted by means of a pressure differential mechanism. A well tapping a geological trap containing oil and/or gas under pressure (proportionate to depth) creates a point of relatively low pressure, so that the fluids in the reservoir all tend to flow toward and into the well, thence to the surface. It follows that if there are two or more owners of land over the reservoir, a well drilled on one property can drain oil or gas from beneath that of the other owners. In an unregulated setting, then, every owner is motivated to drill wells densely, especially along property lines, to extract the mineral(s) at capacity, to flare gas and store oil in open pits pending pipeline construction, and thus quickly to exhaust the expulsion mechanism and with it the economic viability of continued extraction. The general result is massive waste of labor, capital and otherwise economically recoverable minerals, a side effect being temporary depression of prices if the discovery is large relative to the size of the market.

It is important to add that since the waste just described in the case of any given discovery lowers the expected value of any new discovery, it significantly reduces the profitable volume of exploratory effort. Consequently, there is additional waste in the form of "stuff" that might have been converted to resources— might have replenished spent reserves at a given real price—but is left in the ground unfound.

A moment's reflection makes it evident that the problem stems from that bundle of rights we call property. In those parts of the world whose laws stem from the English, minerals in the ground belong to the owners of the surface lying over them. This creates no particular problem if the minerals are naturally immobile, as in the cases of coal and metal bearing ores. But it creates an obvious problem in the cases of oil and gas, especially if an owner has no way of identifying what units of mineral may have been drawn from beneath his/her land by a neighbor. As is well known, the courts "settled" this problem on the analogy of property in wild game, asserting that the property right to extracted oil or gas belongs to the person who recovers them through wells located on his/her land, regardless of where they may have come from.[14]

While it settled the ownership issue, this legal doctrine created—or rather legitimized behavior creating—the waste issue described above. Given the enormous and undeniable waste of labor, capital and minerals, plus the associated functionless instability of prices, the governmental units having jurisdiction (the states in the United States) slowly and painfully moved toward some form of regulation in the name of conservation. As Zimmermann explains, the states faced two contending approaches to regulation. Recognizing that operation of each reservoir as a unit, costs and revenues being shared by prior contract, would remove the rivalry among owners that leads to excessive drilling, rapid extraction and early abandonment, the states could have required such operation as a condition of any extraction at all. They chose, instead, the approach of directly regulating well spacing and maximum production rates per well, no doubt in part because they perceived a need, in the midst of the Great Depression, when regulation finally became universal in the major producing states, to stabilize prices as well as prevent the waste of resources. To head off charges of cartelization, they rationalized price stabilization as an incidental result of preventing "physical" waste and conserving oil and gas resources; and the courts accepted this rationalization.[15] As will be explained below, the states' choice of regulatory approach was the inferior one.

In the 1951 edition of *WRI*, Zimmermann correctly defines the regulatory issues and alternatives, and accurately records the history leading up to the states' choice; but he takes no definite position on what his preference would have been, concluding vaguely: "At present, the situation seems only partially solved; much has been done that points in the right direction, but much still needs to be done" (Zimmermann 1951, p. 536). This seems to suggest that he is uneasy with what had been done but unable or unwilling to say precisely what more should be done. We shall revisit the matter after examining Zimmermann's view on the meaning of conservation.

To sum up this section, we have here a vivid example of the active role of technology in creating resources and the inhibitory role of an institution ill adapted to the efficient utilization of those resources. Technological progress not only effectively created new sources of inanimate energy in the forms of oil and gas, but has thus far continually created new effective supplies of them to replace those used up. But an element in the law underlying the institution of private property, which presented no problem in connection with wood and coal as fuels, had to be adapted to the new situation. That adaptation, the "rule of capture," based on precedent rather than innovation, legitimized behavior leading to massive waste—effectively destruction of resources—which, in turn, led to further modification of property rights in the form of regulation of well spacing and extraction rates. That the process of institutional adaptation, still imperfect, required many decades to be accomplished suggests the magnitude of the welfare losses that can arise from institutional rigidity acting as an impediment to full enjoyment of the potential benefits of dynamic technology.[16]

VI.   ZIMMERMANN ON CONSERVATION

Although technology and facilitating institutional adjustments can create resources, both qualitatively and quantitatively, nature does impose an outer limit on what can be created from given types of neutral stuff; there is only so much raw material out of which to create anything. There accordingly remains a sufficient reason to be concerned about wasteful use of the natural endowment, including an inappropriate intertemporal allocation of natural materials that are nonrenewable. Hence the issue of conservation.

Following a discussion of the history of conservation movements in the United States, and of the various meanings that have been assigned to the term itself, including the vacuous "wise use,"[17] Zimmermann defines conservation as "any act reducing the rate of consumption or exhaustion for the *avowed* purpose of benefiting posterity." (Emphasis added.) (Zimmermann 1951, p. 807). Note two things about this definition. First, the word "avowed" suggests that conservation has to do with intentions, not necessarily effects. Thus the monopolist who reduces current output to raise the price of a resource is not "conserving" it, even though his actions may make more of it available to posterity. Second, there is nothing in this definition to suggest that any net benefit to society is necessarily implied— that there is some optimal degree of reduction in current consumption. By defining conservation in this way, Zimmermann seems to be placing himself into the camp of those who regard conservation as an *ethical* act based on considerations transcending the mere economic. This, in turn, seems to reflect his sense that the pursuit of profit in a market-directed economy is often inconsistent with proper regard for posterity.

He is well aware of the economist's concern for balancing current sacrifice against future benefit, quoting R. T. Ely and L. C. Gray on the matter.

Ely's quoted words:

> Conservation means a sacrifice of the present generation to future generations, whenever it is carried far; this conflict [between current sacrifice and future benefit] beginning far before the ideal is reached which conservationists are inclined to advocate (Zimmermann 1951, p. 805)[18]

Gray's quoted words:

> The primary problem of conservation, expressed in economic language, is the determination of the proper rate of discount on the future with respect to the utilization of our natural resources (Gray 1913, p. 515).

Implying that points of view different from his must be respected, Zimmermann's solution is to make a distinction between conservation as he defines it and what he calls "economization." The latter term is defined as,

...all of the efforts to improve the economic ratio of production, the ratio of output to input, or, expressed socially, the ratio of benefit to sacrifice, of utilities produced to labor expended (Zimmermann 1951, p. 807).

Thus, to Zimmermann, the weighing of future benefits against present sacrifice belongs in the realm of "economization" rather than "conservation."

This point then leads Zimmermann to define two other concepts of his own invention: "conservancy," which is a reduction in current consumption "not sought for its own sake but is incidental to the exercise of economy;" and "economancy," which is "the by-product economy that results incidentally from conservation (Zimmermann 1951, p. 807). These definitions further emphasize the fact that he thought of conservation *per se* as a noneconomic act, although it might have some good economic consequences, just as economic acts *per se* might have some good conservation consequences. "Conservation," in his view, is driven by ethical considerations, "economization" by considerations of material gain.

The distinctions being made here are confusing at best and misleading at worst. Surely the conservation ethic, which holds that we owe to future generations a standard of living at least as high as our own, refers to material wellbeing. To provide for that, we must compare how much we raise the future standard of living with how much we reduce our own by "conserving" resources subject to our control. Furthermore, these distinctions seem to ignore Zimmermann's own dynamic theory of resources. They ignore the fact that there are ways of providing for the future other than reducing the current consumption of natural resources. These ways can be placed under the general rubric of "investment," especially if we define the term broadly, as we should, to include the formation of human capital and knowledge capital as well as the more familiar physical capital. Indeed, it is the substitutability at the margin of such investment for current restraint of natural resource consumption that justifies the discounting of the future benefits of such restraint: the marginal rate of return on capital is the opportunity cost of postponing natural resource consumption.

We have earlier seen, in discussing the concept of "reserves" of depletable resources and the role of concurrent investments in exploration and R & D in replenishing them, that Zimmermann fully appreciated the necessary relationship between decisions to slow down or speed up the rate of extraction and decisions to increase or decrease the rate of replenishing investments. That same relationship exists between extraction rate decisions and all other kinds of investment decisions.

Consider, for example, the effect of a general desire to increase future consumption capabilities by saving more in the present. An increase in the general propensity to save lowers the real rate of interest, *cet par*. A correspondingly lower real rate of discount encourages more capital investment by increasing the present value of expected net proceeds. It also encourages the owners of depletable natural resources, for the same reason, to shift planned rates of extraction toward the future, while simultaneously increasing the level of investment in the search for replacement reserves. All three of these interrelated reactions serve to implement the assumed general desire to shift some consumption from present to future. If there is an impediment to any one of the reactions, the full potential for increasing future consumption capabilities will not be realized, since each interacts with the others.

For another example, consider what happens when it is perceived that the demand for a particular depletable resource will grow at a faster rate than previously expected. This perception translates into the expectation that the relative price of the resource will rise at a faster rate. Given the rate of discount, therefore, the present value of existing reserves of the resource can be increased by shifting some extraction toward the future. At the same time, the prospective profitability of investments in exploration and intensified development is increased. The full adjustments to the original change thus lead to enhanced future extraction, partly at the expense of current extraction, because the market has signalled that consumers will in future place a higher value on the resource than previously expected.

Another part of the adjustment will be the diversion of some capital from other industries to the extraction of the resource in question.

These examples show that choices concerning the intertemporal allocation of depletable resources cannot be logically separated from investment decisions, that the criteria guiding the two kinds of decisions are identical. Indeed, they show that if we really wish to provide future generations with consumption capabilities equal to our own, and do it without unnecessary sacrifice to ourselves, it is in everyone's interest to view the "conservation" of natural resources as an integral part of a more general program of investment in the future. Despite Zimmermann's misgivings on the matter, "conservation," properly viewed, *is* an investment, not a sentimental gift to posterity. So viewed, as L. C. Gray (1913) anticipated H. Hotelling (1931) in pointing out, the optimal intertemporal allocation of a depletable resource—the optimal degree of conservation—is that which maximizes its discounted present value.

We shall return to this point as it bears on the petroleum industry in the next following section. But first, I wish to emphasize that the point is in no way inconsistent with Zimmermann's more general view of the nature of resources, of their creation and destruction. On the contrary. In his chapter on conservation, Zimmermann briefly mentions, but inadequately develops, the connection between his dynamic concept of resources and the problem of conservation (Zimmermann 1951, pp. 809-810). If technological progress can in effect create new natural resources and greater supplies of existing ones, one cannot separate the problem of the rate of use of existing stocks from the expected increases in both recoverable stocks and possible substitutes resulting from such progress. The same is true of expected reduction in institutional constraints. In either case, the positive dynamics of resourceship should have the effect of shifting planned rates of extraction from existing stocks toward the present. In other words, the positive dynamics reduce the degree of current sacrifice associated with appropriate provision for the future. Such provision becomes as much a problem of investing in knowledge creation (research) and human capital formation (education and training) as a problem of the intertemporal allocation of the extraction and use of the resources themselves.

Zimmermann's dynamic view of resources also provides a satisfying answer to the ethical question, What do we owe future generations? Most would say that we owe them a standard of living at least as high as our own. But in the static view of resources, we cannot both use depletable resources and pass on to posterity the ability to produce such a standard of living unless population declines sufficiently. Conservation, in this view, can only slow the decline in either per capita real incomes or population. In the dynamic view, in contrast, we can pass on the same or larger *productive powers* per capita—especially if population growth is restrained—but in the form of a different *mix* of knowledge, human capital, physical capital and natural resources. We may not be able to pass on the same stock of effective petroleum resources, for instance, but we *can* pass on the same stock of effective *energy* resources. As Zimmermann succinctly put it toward the end of his chapter on conservation,

> If.....birth control or other forces hold population growth in check, improved arts and increased knowledge may actually compensate posterity for its reduced supply of material resources[19] (Zimmermann 1951, p. 810).

VII. ZIMMERMANN'S *CONSERVATION IN THE PRODUCTION OF PETROLEUM*

In his final book, published in 1957, Zimmermann undertook to apply his insights into resourceship and conservation to a practical problem of "industrial control"—the problem of regulating the production of oil and gas in the public interest. As earlier explained, he recognized in the 1951 edition of *WRI* that a public policy of *laissez faire* resulted in massive waste of labor, capital and potential resources, as well as in great instability of prices, producer incomes and investment designed to replenish spent reserves. He further recognized there that the states had two general alternatives available to deal with this problem: either (1) require individual reservoirs to be operated as units, thereby removing operators' rivalrous incentives to overdrill and extract at excessive rates, or (2) directly regulate the spacing of wells and their production rates, thereby restraining operators from responding to the incentives. He did not at that time evaluate these alternatives in great depth and chose not to express a preference. Now, in this final study, he was to do both. The real issue addressed was whether to change the states' manner of regulation in response to criticism, since they had long ago (in the late 'twenties and early 'thirties) committed themselves to the second route.

With his characteristic thoroughness, Zimmermann traced in detail the evolution of the prevailing system of conservation regulation, appropriately placing emphasis on "the struggle between Henry L. Doherty and the majority of the directors of the American Petroleum Institute" (Zimmermann 1957, p. 134).[20] Doherty argued for Federal regulation based on unit operation of reservoirs, while the Institute argued for regulation of well spacing and production rates by the several states. Although the Federal Oil Conservation Board[21] held that the Federal government had no constitutional jurisdiction, it did lend moral support to Doherty. With apparent approval, Zimmermann quotes the Board from its fourth report (May 1930) as follows:

> Self-regulation in handling of an oil pool means both efficiency in development and operation and the determination of equities among the owners, and this can best be accomplished by unit operation. By this plan only can each and every owner secure full economic benefits. By this plan only can the public be assured of the largest possible supply of oil and gas from a particular field, won from the ground at lowest cost, and over a period measured by market demand rather than fixed by individualistic greed.[22]

Of the conflict between Doherty and the Institute, Zimmermann cogently observes:

If the avoidance of unprofitable price declines caused by a temporary surplus is identified with stabilization, and if elimination of waste and the increase in the amount of ultimate recovery are associated with the idea of conservation, one can summarize this discussion by saying that the industry, if it is considered as being represented by its chief spokesmen at that time, was concerned mainly with what some have called stabilization, and Doherty mainly with conservation (Zimmermann 1957a, p. 135).

Since Zimmermann was presumably concerned mainly with conservation and seemed to approve of the Federal Conservation Board's comments quoted above, one would expect him to come down on the side of regulation by means of compulsory unitization *cum* manager freedom. Alas, it was not to be. The reason why is traceable in part to his belief, explained in the previous section, that conservation and efficiency are not the same thing and can be opposed to each other; and in part to his distrust of the free market allocative mechanism, especially in its intertemporal dimension. He could not bring himself to accept the arguments of Gray (1913), Ciriacy-Wantrup (1952) and Hotelling (1931) that conservation (at least its degree) properly means efficient intertemporal allocation, and that firms motivated by the desire to maximize profits can be trusted to conserve resources to the socially optimal degree, *provided all social costs and benefits are internalized.* (Present writer's emphasis.)

Consider his peremptory dismissal of Ciriacy-Wantrup:

> Unfortunately, his definition of the optimum state of conservation for social policy as that state of conservation which 'maximizes social net revenues over time' amounts to little more than a substitution of mathematical symbols for the solution of the real problems of policy making (Zimmermann 1957a, p. 31).[23]

Zimmermann then goes on to say:

> It is the legitimate function, indeed the duty, of the economist to point out what action appears economically sound and unsound to him. But he is not the sole judge and final arbiter of policies society may adopt in matters *other than* purely economic. (Emphasis added.) (Zimmermann, 1957a, p. 32)

In other words, "conservation" is to Zimmermann something distinct from economic efficiency.

As for petroleum conservation specifically, Zimmermann appeals to Harold Hotelling, ironically a member of the "maximization of present value" school, for support of the view that (in Zimmermann's words) "petroleum possesses characteristics which interfere drastically with such orthodox planning for the maximization of present values" (Zimmermann 1957a, p. 30). It is true that Hotelling explicitly excluded oil and gas production from his general conclusion that government intervention is not needed to ensure the conservation of depletable resources. He did so, however, for the specific reason that the fugitive-resource, common-pool problem means that in the absence of some form of government intervention operators do not bear the full social costs of current extraction (Hotelling 1931, p. 144).[24] The cost of necessity ignored is what is now known as "user cost," that is, the present value of future net revenues forgone. The unregulated operator cannot take this social cost into account because to him/her a unit of oil or gas not produced today is a unit lost to a neighbor, not one that can be held in the ground to be extracted by him/her at some future date. What Zimmermann fails to perceive is that unitized operation of a reservoir effectively internalizes this social cost, so that the desire of the operator to maximize present value is fully consistent with society's interest in conservation.[25]

I believe that if Zimmermann had fully understood Hotelling—if he had recognized the concept of user cost, which if external can be internalized—he would have been less critical of profit maximization as the principle of allocative efficiency and less inclined toward his conclusion in favor of the prevailing system of regulation of the oil and gas industry.

It is clear that Zimmermann struggled in reaching that conclusion. He definitely recognized the technical superiority of unitized operations. But another consideration—stabilization—weighed heavily in his thinking. The disaster of the Great Depression was never far from his mind, and he had a certain sympathy for the New Deal policies that sought to stabilize prices—for farmers, industrialists and petroleum producers—by restricting production and allocating the total among producers by quota. He could argue that the instability of oil and gas prices, by creating unnecessary uncertainty, was itself a barrier to rational utilization of the resources in question, especially as regards investments in new exploration and intensified development of known deposits. He evidently felt that the regulation of well spacing and production rates could *both* eliminate the grosser wastes of labor, capital and natural resources otherwise observed *and* produce sufficient price stability to overcome the uncertainty barrier; whereas unitized operation of reservoirs could only accomplish the former.

Again, he fails fully to grasp the implications of Hotelling's argument. If operators are free to arrange the intertemporal schedule of extraction so as to maximize present value at all times, a temporary depression of prices (due, say, to a large discovery, or to a general recession) would induce them to shift some extraction from present to future when prices could be expected to be higher. Similarly, if prices are temporarily elevated (due, say, to a defense emergency) it would be in their interest to shift some planned extraction from the future to the present. These responses to unusually low or high prices, generalized to all producers, would tend obviously to stabilize prices. And this method of stabilizing prices, unlike the general regulation of extraction rates by the state authorities, would not lend itself to permanent restriction of production in order to raise the price above its competitive level.[26]

It is true that Zimmermann was somewhat uneasy about his conclusion in favor of the prevailing system of regulation. He devotes an entire chapter (Ch. 10) to the "weaknesses and unsolved problems" of the system. In the final paragraphs of his summary and conclusions he cautions the reader:

> .....It must be clearly understood that this endorsement, while unequivocal in its general conclusion, is by no means complete and definitive. Although much improved over earlier versions, the system of control now extant is still far from perfect..... The endorsement here given retains its validity only so long as the basic conditions underlying and affecting the industry remain essentially as here described for the period over which this analysis extends.

Above all, the endorsement rests on an effort to strike a balance
between pros and cons as regards many phases and issues underlying
the major controversy. Such a balance can be struck only by applying
subjective personal judgment to many complex questions and then
searching for a final conclusion out of this welter of personal judgments
(Zimmermann 1957a, p. 394).

Today, the "basic conditions underlying and affecting the
industry" *are* quite different. OPEC now effectively controls
the world price, and the domestic oil (not gas) industry is being
rapidly liquidated. I think that today Zimmermann would
reach a different conclusion. Not least among his considerations would be recently developed evidence of the enormous
cost imposed upon American society by the extant system,
which has not been changed in any fundamental way since
Zimmermann wrote, in comparison with the alternative of
universal unitized operations *cum* manager freedom. In April,
1994, the Bureau of Economic Analysis, U.S. Department of
Commerce, published the results of its efforts to measure the
value of the nation's mineral resources with a view to
incorporating a measure of their depletion into the national
accounts.[27] Two basic methods of estimating reserve values
were employed, with several variations. The first basic method
employs the valuation principle based on Hotelling: if
operators are free to arrange intertemporal schedules of
extraction rates so as to maximize profits, the in-ground value
per unit should be equal to the concurrent market price net
of marginal extraction costs. The other basic method is simply
to use actual sales prices of reserves, these actual prices
presumably reflecting the expectation that extraction rates
would continue to be regulated as per the extant system.
Comparable estimates are available for the years 1977 through
1991, and the pattern observed is consistent for the whole
period. I shall therefore cite the figures for the terminal year
only. By the Hotelling-based method, the year-end value of oil
reserves was $126.8 billion. By the actual transaction price
method, the value was $45.1 billion, 65 percent less.[28] Since
investments in exploration and intensified development are

undertaken on the basis of the expected value of what may be found and proved, it is clear that the rapid decline in domestic production since 1970, checked only briefly during the years of extraordinarily high real prices, 1978-1985, owes much to the high costs unnecessarily imposed on the industry by the system of regulation endorsed somewhat uneasily by Zimmermann in 1957. To repeat, I think he would not give his endorsement today.

VIII. CONCLUSIONS

The above criticisms of Zimmermann's views on conservation, based partly on hindsight, do not detract in any way from his brilliant dynamic theory of resourceship. It is this theory that represents his great and lasting contribution to economic thought; and if his excursions into matters of public policy leave something to be desired, it is, in my opinion, because he fails fully to exploit the unique insights of his own theory. If, as he rightly perceives, resources are the creation of human societies, "conservation" has a much broader meaning than merely slowing the current rate of use of particular varieties of resources, such as oil and gas. It means the integration of rate-of-use decisions with those of investments in capital formation, the latter broadly defined to include the creation of new knowledge and its dissemination, as well as additions to the stock of physical capital. It is *this whole* of future oriented decisions that determines the welfare potential of posterity, not any single part of it.

It has never been more important to understand this point than today. In recent decades, knowledge ("the mother of all other resources") and its dissemination have come to the fore in growth and development theory; and the externalities associated with incomplete specification and assignment of property rights have come to the fore in environmental economics.[29] The latter point recalls Zimmermann's recognition of the impediments inappropriately adjusted institutions may impose on the otherwise dynamic processes of resource creation and economic growth. Proposals to measure and internalize externalities by means of market-based instruments, such as tradable permits, are proposals to modify property rights in such a way as to integrate environmental protection measures, obviously an aspect of "conservation," with the whole complex of decisions affecting the current and intertemporal allocation of productive resources. Zimmermann's dynamic theory of resourceship allows us to see what he calls the "altogetherness" (Zimmermann 1957a, p. 818) of all the circumstances and processes determining our present and future welfare, hence to appreciate the value of integrating the processes of allocative decision-making.

The reader of this volume will readily see the connections between Zimmermann's teaching and that of others in the "Texas School," especially Ayres, Wiley and Montgomery, but not excluding Hale and Allen. Would he have called himself an "institutionalist?" I never heard him do so; but in a document Zimmermann wrote for a news release in 1957, announcing the imminent publication of his last book, he characterized himself as "a pioneer in stressing the functional *and institutional* approach in the study of human, material, and intangible resources." (Emphasis added.)[30] But a label is not the point. The point is that institutionalists and orthodox economists alike can still find in Zimmermann's work inspiration and guidance for research into some of the most challenging social problems of the age.

ACKNOWLEDGMENTS

The author gratefully acknowledges the assistance and helpful comments of Gerald F. Vaughn, particularly in regard to Zimmermann's biographical data, but also in regard to book reviews and other published materials about him.

NOTES

1. For other sources relating Zimmermann to the "Texas School" see: Gordon, Wendell and John Adams, *Economics as Social Science: An*

Evolutionary Approach (Riverdale, MD: The Riverdale Company, 1989) pp. 34-37; Dugger, Wm. M., "A Research Agenda for Institutional Economics," in Dugger (Ed.), *Radical Institutionalism: Contemporary Voices* (New York: Greenwood Press, 1989) pp. 114-17; and De Gregori, Thos. R., "Technology and Ceremonial Behavior: Aspects of Institutionalism," *Journal of Economic Issues*, Vol. 11 (1977), No. 4, pp. 867-68.

2. The data in this section are derived from several sources, including *In Memoriam: Erich Walter Zimmermann*, memorial resolution prepared by a committee composed of Calvin P. Blair, chairman, Clarence E. Ayres and Stanley A. Arbingast, and filed with the Secretary of the General Faculty, The University of Texas, July 13, 1966; Howell, A. C., *The Kenan Professorships* (Chapel Hill: The University of North Carolina, 1956) pp. 340-43; and "Erich W. Zimmermann," text of the encomium on the occasion of Zimmermann's induction into the Hall of Fame, College of Business Administration, The University of Texas, 1985. As noted in the acknowledgment section, most of the data were provided to the present writer by Gerald F. Vaughn.

3. Rainey, Homer P., Letter to members of the Board of Regents, The University of Texas, May 15, 1940.

4. Rainey, Homer P., Letter to members of the Board of Regents, The University of Texas, November 12, 1941.

5. This and the following five paragraphs summarize the first three chapters of *WRI*.

6. Cf. Douglass C. North's definition of "institution" in *Institutions, Institutional Change and Economic Performance* (Cambridge: Cambridge University Press, 1990), p. 3. "Institutions.....are the humanly devised constraints that shape human interaction." And in further explanation, p. 6: "The major role of institutions in a society is to reduce uncertainty by establishing a stable (but not necessarily efficient) structure to human interaction."

7. See essay on Ayres, this volume.

8. Zimmermann devotes a whole "unit" (Ch. 4-6) to this subject.

9. See essay on Wiley, this volume.

10. Most of the points in this paragraph were made in Clarence A. Wiley's only book, *Agriculture and the Business Cycle Since 1920: A Study in the Postwar Disparity of Prices*, No. 15 in Studies in the Social Sciences and History (Madison: The University of Wisconsin, 1930). Zimmermann does not refer to this book, but he does refer to works by Theodore Schultz and D. Gale Johnson in which similar points are made, and with which all of Wiley's students would have been familiar.

11. Wiley's students would have been familiar with this point also. In fact, it was the major theme of Wiley's lectures, as well as of Schultz' and Johnson's works.

12. This and the following seven paragraphs summarize Chapters 25 and 32 of *WRI*.

13. Historically, the U. S. petroleum industry has recovered an average of about 30 percent of the oil originally in place in discovered reservoirs. However, the percentage has steadily increased, especially since the 1920's, due to technological progress and regulation.

14. The "rule of capture" originates with *Westmoreland Natural Gas Company v. DeWitt* (130 Pa. 235, 18 Atl. 724, 1889).

15. *Champlin Refining Company v. Oklahoma Corporation Commission* (52 S.Ct. 559, 1932).

16. See below for a recent estimate of a measure of welfare loss.

17. As Zimmermann observes, the real question is, What is wise? *WRI*, p. 805.

18. The quotation is from Ely, R. T., "Conservation and Economic Theory," Part I of Ely, R. T., R. H. Hess, C. K. Leith, and T. N. Carver, *The Foundations of National Prosperity: Studies in the Conservation of Permanent National Resources.* (New York: The Macmillan Company 1923), p. 33.

19. For a reflection of the optimism that can follow from Zimmermann's dynamic theory of resourceship, see Julian L. Simon, *The Ultimate Resource* (Princeton: Princeton University Press 1981), especially chapters 3-10. Simon's "ultimate resource" turns out to be the same as Zimmermann's "mother of all other resources," to wit: knowledge. (Simon, *op.cit.*, p. 222.)

20. Doherty was fiscal agent of the Cities Service Companies and president of H. L. Doherty and Company.

21. Appointed by President Coolidge in 1924 to study the oil conservation problem in relation to the national interest.

22. Fourth report of the Federal Oil Conservation Board, (May 1930) pp.17-24, quoted by Zimmermann, 1957a, 132.

23. The part of this sentence quoting Ciriacy-Wantrup omits the words "the present value of" following the word "maximizes."

24. Regarding government intervention, see Libecap, G. D. and S. N. Wiggins (1984). They explain why early efforts to deal with the common pool problem via private contracts among operators generally failed in the absence of government enforcement.

25. When user cost is taken into account, the complete marginal cost of current extraction is the sum of marginal extraction cost and marginal user cost, where the latter is the present value of net revenues forgone at any time in future by virtue of the last unit of current extraction.

26. Economists' usual criticism of the regulatory system in practice was (until control of price passed to OPEC) that it was in fact used to raise the price of oil above its competitive level by artificially restricting total domestic production and allocating it among otherwise competing producers.

27. *Survey of Current Business,* April 1994, pp. 32-72.

28. *Ibid.,* pp. 65 and 67.

29. Zimmermann does not address in *WRI* the problems we today associate with environmental degradation. In his terms, such degradation might be viewed as "destruction" of resources due in part to institutional impediments; and it raises the question of whether technology can "create" substitute resources to replace those being destroyed. For a discussion of this issue, see Swaney, James A. (1985) also his "Elements of a Neoinstitutional Environmental Economics" in Marc R. Tool (ed.), *Evolutionary Economics,* Vol. II (Armonk, NY: M. E. Sharpe, Inc. 1988) pp. 321-40.

30. Courtesy of News and Information Services, The University of Texas.

Bibliography

Agee, J., and Walker E. 1941. *Let Us Now Praise Famous Men*. Boston: Houghton Mifflin.

Allen, R. A. 1933. *The Labor of Women in the Production of Cotton*. Ph.D. Dissertation, The University of Chicago, published in 1975 by Arno Press.

———. 1941. *Chapters in the History of Organized Labor in Texas*. The University of Texas Publication, No. 4143.

———. 1942. *The Great Southwest Strike*. The University of Texas Publication, No. 4214.

———. 1952: Ten entries in *Handbook of Texas*, Volumes I and II, edited by W.P Webb and H.B. Carroll. Texas State Historical Association, Austin.

———. 1961. *East Texas Lumber Workers: An Economic and Social Picture, 1870-1850*. Austin: University of Texas Press.

Armstrong, A. B. M. 1934. *The Administrative Set-Up of the A. A. A.*, M.A. thesis. Austin: University of Texas.

Ayres, C. E. 1944. *The Theory of Economic Progress*. Chapel Hill: University of North Carolina.

———. 1946. *The Divine Right of Capital*. Boston: Houghton-Mifflin.

———. 1952a. *The Industrial Economy*. Boston: Houghton-Mifflin.

———. 1952b. "The Integration of Industrial Society." Pp. 165-177 in *The Cleavage in Our Culture: Studies in Scientific Humanism in Honor of Max Otto*, edited by Frederick Burkhardt. Boston: Beacon.

———. 1961. *Toward a Reasonable Society*. Austin: University of Texas Press.

———. 1962. *The Theory of Economic Progress*. New York: Schocken.

———. 1964. "The Legacy of Thorstein Veblen." Pp. 45-62 in *Institutional Economics: Veblen, Commons, and Mitchell Reconsidered*. Berkeley: University of California Press.

———. 1966. "Guaranteed Income: An Institutionalist View." Pp. 169-182 in *The Guaranteed Income*, edited by R. Theobald. Garden City, NY: Doubleday.

———. 1967. "Ideological Responsibility." *Journal of Economic Issues*. 1 (June): 3-11.

Bain, J. 1949. "A Note on Pricing in Monopoly and Oligopoly." *American Economic Review* 39: 448-464.

Beckwith, B. P. 1955. *Marginal-Cost Price-Output Control.* New York: Columbia University Press.

Bedichek, R. 1944. Letter to Dan Williams, December 28. In *Letters of Roy Bedichek,* edited by William A. Owens and Lyman Grant. Austin: University of Texas, 1985.

————— . 1956. *Educational Competition: The Story of the University Interscholastic League of Texas.* Austin: University of Texas.

Benedict, H. Y. 1929. Letter to Edmund T. Miller, September 3.

Blair, C. P. et al., 1966. *In Memoriam: Erich Walter Zimmermann.* Memorial resolution filed with Office of the General Faculty, The University of Texas at Austin (mimeo.)

Blaug, M. 1983. *Economic Theory in Retrospect.* 4th ed. New York: Cambridge University Press.

Bowles, S., Gordon, D., and Weisskopf, T. 1983. *Beyond the Waste Land.* Garden City, NY: Anchor Press.

Breit, W. 1970. "Some Early Unconventional Wisdom on Utility Regulation," *Social Science Quarterly* 50: 859-886.

————— . 1973. "The Development of Clarence Ayres's Theoretical Institutionalism." *Social Science Quarterly* 54: 244-57.

————— . 1987. "Creating the 'Virginia School': Charlottesville as an Academic Environment in the 1960s," *Economic Inquiry* 25 (October): 645.

————— . 1988. "Institutional Economics as an Ideological Movement." In *Philosophy, History and Social Action,* edited by S. Hook, W. L. O'Neill, and R. O'Toole, Kluwer Academic Publishers.

Breit, W., and William P. C., Jr., (eds.) 1976. *Science and Ceremony: The Institutional Economics of C. E. Ayres.* Austin: University of Texas Press.

Ciriacy-Wantrup, S. V. 1952. *Resource Conservation: Economics and Policies.* Berkeley: University of California Press.

Daily Texan. 1943. Austin: University of Texas student newspaper, July 29.

Daily Texan. 1945. September 26.

De Gregori, T. R. 1977. "Technology and Ceremonial Behavior: Aspects of Institutionalism." *Journal of Economic Issues,* 11(4): 861-70.

Dewey, J. 1948. *Reconstruction in Philosophy.* (Enlarged ed). Boston: Beacon.

Dillard. D. 1987. "Money as an Institution of Capitalism." *Journal of Economic Issues* 21(December): 1623-1647.

Dugger, W. M. 1989a. "A Research Agenda for Institutional Economics" in ————— . (ed.) *Radical Institutionalism: Contemporary Voices.* New York: Greenwood Press.

————— . 1989b. *Radical Institutionalism.* New York: Greenwood Press.

————— . 1989c. *Corporate Hegemony.* New York: Greenwood Press.

Dugger, W.M., and W.T. Waller, Jr., eds. 1992. *The Stratified State*. Armonk, NY: M.E. Sharpe.

Dugger, R. 1974. *Our Invaded Universities: Form, Reform, and New Starts*. New York: W. W. Norton.

Duval, C. A. 1932. *Basic Farm Reform*, Ph.D. dissertation. Austin: University of Texas.

Ely, R. T. 1884. "The Past and the Present of Political Economy." Pp. 1-64 in *Johns Hopkins University Studies in Historical and Political Science*, Vol. II, edited by Herbert B. Adams, Part III. Baltimore: Johns Hopkins University.

————. 1889. *An Introduction to Political Economy*. New York: Chautauqua.

————. 1923. "Conservation and Economic Theory" in Ely, R. T. et al., *The Foundations of National Prosperity: Studies in the Conservation of Permanent National Resources*. New York: The Macmillan Company.

————. 1938. *Ground Under Our Feet*. New York: MacMillan.

Ely, R. T., Shine, M. L., and Wehrwein, G. S. 1922. *Outlines of Land Economics* (three volumes). Ann Arbor: Edwards Brothers.

Erickson, M. n.d. "The Economics of R.H. Montgomery" (unpublished).

Evans, B. M. n.d. "The Economics of C. A. Wiley" (unpublished) draft of paper presented at annual meeting of Southwestern Social Science Association.

Evans, B. M. 1954. *Institutional Inhibitors To Adequate Farm Size Adjustment*, M.A. thesis. Austin: University of Texas.

Ezekiel, M. 1932. "Review of *Agriculture and the Business Cycle Since 1920: A Study in the Post-War Disparity of Prices*" *The Journal of Political Economy* 40(1932):420-421.

Foster, J. F. 1981. "The Approach to Land Use Planning in a Changing Technology." *Journal of Economic Issues* 15: 985-1007.

Galbraith, J. K. 1958. *The Affluent Society*. Boston: Houghton-Mifflin.

————. 1967. *The New Industrial State*. Boston: Houghton-Mifflin.

Galbraith, J. K. 1973a. "Power and the Useful Economist." *American Economic Review*. 63 (March): 1-11.

————. 1973b. *Economics and the Public Purpose*. Boston: Houghton-Mifflin.

Garnett, W. E. 1923. *Some Socially Significant Rural Conditions*. Bulletin of the Agricultural and Mechanical College of Texas, Third Series, *9*(9): (Also identified as Rural Sociology Publication No. 2).

Glaeser, M. 1927. *Outlines of Public Utility Economics* New York: Macmillan.

Gordon, W., Miller, D., and Morgan, D. C. 1975. "In Memorium: Edward Everett Hale" Pp. 11807-11811 in *Documents and Minutes of the General Faculty*, Austin: The University of Texas Press.

Gordon, W. C., and Adams, J. 1989. *Economics as Social Science: An Evolutionary Approach*. Riverdale, MD: The Riverdale Company.

Gray, L. C. 1913. "Economic Possibilities of Conservation." *Quarterly Journal of Economics*, 27(3): 497-519.

Green, G. N. 1979. *The Establishment in Texas Politics: The Primitive Years, 1938-1957.* Norman: University of Oklahoma Press.

Hale, E. E. n.d. "Keynes: General Theory of Employment, Interest, and Money." (unpublished).

_____. n.d. *Lecture Notes on Marx, Jevons, and Marshall* (unpublished).

_____. c1926. "Metaphysics, Science, and Value Theory," Paper written for Economics 144 at the University of Wisconsin, and taught by John R. Commons.

_____. 1933. "The Problem of Monetary Standards" (unpublished).

_____. 1937. "Fascism vs. Communism" *Southwestern Social Science Quarterly*, (June): 15-24.

_____. 1939. "Review of *Economics and Society* by Cronin," *Southwestern Social Science Quarterly* (December).

_____. 1942. "Economic Pattern of a Durable Peace" (unpublished).

_____. 1945. "Review of *Readings in Business Cycle Theory.*" *The Journal of Land and Public Utility Economics* 21: 298-299.

_____. c1947. "Review of *The New Economics*, edited by Seymour E. Harris," (unpublished).

_____. 1976. "Some Implications of Keynes' *General Theory, of Employment Interest and Money.*" *Review of Radical Political Economics* 8 (Winter): 30-41.

Hamilton, W. H. 1919. "The Institutional Approach to Economic Theory." *American Economic Review.* 9 (March): 309-18.

_____. 1957. *The Politics of Industry.* New York: A.A. Knopf.

Hill, F. n.d. "The Economics of Ruth Allen." (unpublished manuscript).

Hotelling, H. 1931. "The Economics of Exhaustible Resources." *Journal of Political Economy* 39(2): 137-75

_____. 1938. "The General Welfare in Relation to Problems of Taxation and of Railway and Utility Rates." *Econometrica* 6: 242-269.

Howell, A. C. 1956. *The Kenan Professorships.* Chapel Hill: The University of North Carolina Press.

Hutchison, T. W. 1981. *The Politics and Philosophy of Economics.* New York: New York University Press.

Jensen, H. n.d. "The Economics of Edward Everett Hale: An Impressionistic Fragment" (unpublished).

Jensen, J. M. 1980. "Cloth, Butter, and Boarders: Women's Household Production for the Market." *Review of Radical Political Economics* 12(2):

Jones, D. N. 1988. "Regulatory Concepts, Propositions and Doctrines: Casualties and Survivors." *Journal of Economic Issues 22*: 1092-1093.

Kahn, A. E. 1988. *The Economics of Regulation: Principles and Institutions.* Cambridge: MIT Press.

Kirkendall, R. S. 1963. "L. C. Gray and the Supply of Agricultural Land." *Agricultural History* 37: 206-216.

Klein, P. 1990. "Institutionalism as a School—A Reconsideration." *Journal of Economic Issues* 24 (June): 381-388.

Krueger, A. O. 1991. "Report of the Commission on Graduate Education in Economics." *Journal of Economic Literature* 29 (September): 1035-1053.

Krugman, P. R. 1990. *Rethinking International Trade*. Cambridge, MA: MIT Press.

————. 1994. *Peddling Prosperity: Economic Sense and Nonsense in the Age of Diminished Expectations*. New York: W.W. Norton.

Land Policy Circular 1936. Land Use Planning Section, Division of Land Utilization, U.S. Resettlement Administration.

Langsam, W. C. 1934. Review of *World Resources and Industries*, 1933. *Political Science Quarterly* 49(3): 457-459.

Libecap, G. D., and Wiggins, S. N. 1984. "Contractual Responses to the Common Pool." *American Economic Review* 74(1): 87-98.

Liebhafsky, H. H., Gordon, W., and Redford, E. 1977. "In Memoriam: Clarence Edwin Ayres." *Journal of Economic Issues*. 11 (September): 475-483.

Lowe, A. 1983. *On Economic Knowledge: Toward a Science of Political Economics*. Second enlarged ed. Armonk, NY: M.E. Sharpe.

Mann, S. 1989. "Slavery, Sharecropping, and Sexual Inequality." in *Signs*, *14*(4).

Markowitz, N. D. 1973. *The Rise and Fall of the People's Century*. New York: Free Press.

Mayhew, A. 1987. "Culture: Core Concept Under Attack." *Journal of Economic Issues* 21: 587-603.

McDonald, S. L. 1992a. Letter to author, August 10.

————. 1992b. Letter to author, August 24.

————. 1993a. Telephone interviews, February 5 and 27.

————. 1993b. Letter to Gerald Vaughn, April 4.

Mertz, P. E. 1978. *New Deal Policy and Southern Rural Poverty*. Baton Rouge: Louisiana State University Press.

Miller, E. T. 1929. Letter to Harry Y. Benedict, August 28.

Montgomery, M. 1937. *The Agricultural Adjustment Administration and the Cotton Farmer*. M.A. thesis. Austin: University of Texas.

Montgomery, R. H. n.d. "Montgomery Talks" unpublished.

————. 1925. "The Interstate Commerce Commission and the General Level of Freight Rates." *Southwestern Social Science Quarterly* (March): 299-326.

————. 1929. *The Cooperative Pattern in Cotton*. New York: MacMillan.

————. 1931a. "The Federal Farm Board: Operating in Cotton." *American Cooperation*, Vol. I. Washington DC: The American Institute of Cooperation.

————— . 1931b. "Judicial Fair Value and the Price Level." *Southwestern Social Science Quarterly* (December): 221-237.

————— . 1939a. "Government Ownership and Operation of the Electric Industry." *Annals of the American Academy of Political and Social Sciences* 20 (January): 43-49.

————— . 1939b. "Government Ownership and Operation of the Railroads." *Annals of the American Academy of Political and Social Sciences* 201 (January): 137-145.

————— . 1940. *The Brimstone Game.* New York: Vanguard.

————— . 1970. "Like It Is: The Impact of Science on Culture." *Social Science Quarterly* 50: 881-886.

Munkirs, J. R. 1983. "Centralized Private Sector Planning: An Institutionalist's Perspective on the Contemporary U.S. Economy." *Journal of Economic Issues* 17 (December): 931-967.

North, D. C. 1990. *Institutions, Institutional Change, and Economic Performance.* Cambridge: Cambridge University Press.

————— . 1994. "Economic Performance Through Time," *American Economic Review* 84: 359-368.

Odum, H. W., and Moore, H. E. 1938. *American Regionalism: A Cultural-Historical Approach to National Integration.* New York: Henry Holt.

————— . 1951. *American Sociology: The Story of Sociology in the United States through 1950.* New York: Longmans, Green and Co.

Patenaude, L. V. 1980. "Texas and the New Deal." Pp. 89-101, in *The Depression in the Southwest,* edited by Donald W. Whisenhunt. Port Washington, NY: Kennikat.

Peach, W. N., and Constantin, J. A. 1972. *Zimmermann's World Resources and Industries,* 3rd Ed. New York: Harper and Row.

Phillips, R. J. 1976. "E. E. Hale on Keynes's *General Theory.*" *Review of Radical Political Economics* 8 (Winter): 30-31.

————— . 1989a. "Radical Institutionalism and the Texas School of Economics." In *Radical Institutionalism: Contemporary Voices,* edited by William M. Dugger. Westport, CT: Greenwood Press.

————— . 1989b. "Is There a Texas School of Economics?" *Journal of Economic Issues 23* (3 September 1989: 863-872.

————— . 1994. "The Texas School of Institutional Economics." In *The Elgar Companion to Institutional and Evolutionary Economics,* edited by Geoffrey M. Hodgson, Warren J. Samuels, and Marc Tool. Brookfield, VT: Edward Elgar Publishing.

Polanyi, K. 1957. *The Great Transformation.* (Pb. edn). Boston: Beacon.

Ranson, B. 1987. "The Institutionalist Theory of Capital Formation." *Journal of Economic Issues.* 21 (September): 1265-78.

Reed, J. S., and Singal, D. J. (eds.) 1982. *Regionalism and the South: Selected Papers of Rupert Vance.* Chapel Hill: University of North Carolina Press.

Richardson, J. 1992a. Letter to Vaughn, September 3.

Richardson, J. 1992b. Telephone interview, October 7.

Rosen, E. A. 1977. *Hoover, Roosevelt, and the Brains Trust: From Depression to New Deal*. New York: Columbia University Press.

Sachs, C. E. 1983. *The Invisible Farmers: Women in Agricultural Production*, Rowman and Allanheld.

Samuels, W. J. 1987. "Clarence Edwin Ayres." In J.M. Eatwell, M. Millgate, and P. Newman. (eds). *The New Palgrave, A Dictionary of Economics*. V. 1. New York: Stockton Press.

Simon, J. L. 1981. *The Ultimate Resource*. Princeton, NJ: Princeton University Press.

Smelser, N. J. 1967. "Toward a Theory of Modernization." Originally published in 1963 and reprinted in *Tribal and Peasant Economies: Readings in Economic Anthropology*, edited by George Dalton, pp. 29-48. Garden City, NY: Natural History Press.

Stanfield, J. R. 1986. *The Economic Thought of Karl Polanyi*. London: Macmillan Press and New York: St. Martin's Press.

————. 1995. *Economics, Power, and Culture: Essays in the Development of Radical Institutionalism*. London: Macmillan.

————. forthcoming. *J.K. Galbraith*. London: MacMillan.

Street, J. H. n.d. "The Associates of C. E. Ayres in the Texas School of Economics." Unpublished draft of paper presented at annual meeting of Southwestern Social Science Association.

Swaney, J. A. 1985. "Economics, Ecology and Entropy." *Journal of Economic Issues* 19(4): 853-65.

————. 1988. "Elements of a Neoinstitutional Environmental Economics." In *Evolutionary Economics*, Vol. II, edited by M. R. Tool. Armonk, NY: M. E. Sharpe, Inc.

Tilman, R. 1987. "The Neoinstrumental Theory of Democracy." *Journal of Economic Issues* 21 (September): 1379-1401.

Tool, M. R. 1979. *The Discretionary Economy*. Santa Monica, CA: Goodyear Press.

————. (ed.), 1988. *Evolutionary Economics*, (2 volumes). Armonk, NY: M. E. Sharpe, Inc.

Tullock, G. 1967. "The Welfare Costs of Tariffs, Monopolies and Theft." *Western Economic Journal* 5: 224-232.

Tyson, L. D. 1993. *Who's Bashing Whom?: Trade Conflicts in High-technology Industries*. Washington, DC: Institute for International Economics.

University of Texas 1917-1922. *Catalogue of the University Summer Schools*. March.

University of Texas 1920-1957. *Catalogue of the University of Texas*. May.

Vaughn, G. F. 1993a. "McDonald and Wiley: Their Hidden Jewels For Ag Policy." *Choices*, American Agricultural Economics Association, (Fourth Quarter): 38-39.

————— . 1993b. "Rural Development in an Integrated Economy." *Network93*, Northeast Regional Center for Rural Development, Jan.-Feb. 1993, pp. 3-4.

————— . 1993c. "Ely, Wiley, and Land Economics in the Integrating Global Economy." *Land Economics* 69: 438-442.

Veblen, T. B. 1904. *The Theory of Business Enterprise*. New York: New American Library.

————— . 1953. [1899]. *The Theory of the Leisure Class*. New York: New American Library.

Vickery, W. 1955. "Some Implications of Marginal Cost Pricing for Public Utilities." *American Economic Review* 45 (May): 605-612.

Viner, J. 1931. "Cost Curves and Supply Curves." *Zeitschrift fur National-okonomie* 3 (1931): 23-46.

Walker, D. A. 1978. "The Economic Policy Proposals of Clarence Ayres." *Southern Economic Journal*. 44 (January): 616-28.

Walter, L. W. 1952-53. Review of *World Resources and Industries*, 1951. *Southwestern Social Science Quarterly*, 33(1): 59-60.

Wells, O. V. 1932. Review of *Agriculture and the Business Cycle Since 1920: A Study in the Post-War Disparity of Prices Journal of Farm Economics* 14(1932):176-179.

Wehrwein, G. S. 1936. News Item in *Journal of Farm Economics* 18: 448.

Wiecking, E. H. 1935. Letter to H. M. Salmon, September 13.

Wiley, C. A. 1924-25. "The Economics and Politics of the Agricultural Tariff." *Southwestern Political and Social Science Quarterly* 5: 264-278.

————— . 1925-26. "Agriculture and the Disparity in Prices." *Southwestern Political and Social Science Quarterly* 6: 336-348.

————— . 1927. "Supply and Demand Factors in the Post-War Agricultural Situation." Annual meetings of the Southwestern Social Science Association.

————— . 1928-29a. Review of Waite: Economics of Consumption. *Southwestern Political and Social Science Quarterly* 9: 499-500.

————— . 1928-29b. Review of Patton: *Diminishing Returns in Agriculture*. *Southwestern Political and Social Science Quarterly* 9: 513-515.

————— . 1929a. Letter to Edmund T. Miller, August 28.

————— . 1929b. "Quality Production as a Factor in Successful Cooperative Marketing." Texas Annual Cooperative Marketing Conference, Texas A&M University.

————— . 1929. "Land Utilization in the Southwest" and discussant of "Mexican Labor in the Southwest." Annual meetings of the Southwestern Social Science Association.

————— . 1930. *Agriculture and the Business Cycle Since 1920: A Study in the Post-War Disparity of Prices*. Studies in the Social Sciences and History, No. 15. Madison: University of Wisconsin.

————— . 1932. "The Future of the Agricultural Price Situation."Annual meetings of the Southwestern Social Science Association.

————— . 1933. "Control Measures for Agricultural Prices: Voluntary Domestic Allotment Plan" and "Some Farm Ownership and Tenancy Problems in Texas." Annual meetings of the Southwestern Social Science Association.

————— . 1934. "The A.A.A. and a Constructive, Long-Time Program for the Livestock Industry." Annual meetings of the Southwestern Social Science Association.

————— . 1936a. Discussion of Rupert B. Vance's paper on "Cotton and Tenancy." Pp. 40-44 in *Problems of the Cotton Economy*. Proceedings of the Southern Social Science Research Conference, New Orleans, March 8-9, 1935. Dallas: Arnold Foundation and Southern Methodist University, 1936a.

————— . 1936b. "Why a Land-Use Program for Florida?" *Florida Grower* 45:(2):5, 24.

————— . 1936c. "Current Farm Problems." Farmers' Short Course, College of Arts and Industries, Kingsville, Texas.

————— . 1937a. "Tenure Problems and Research Needs in the South." *Journal of Farm Economics* 19: 128-139.

————— . 1937b. Comment on "Land Utilization: The Social Aspects of Land Adjustment Problems." *Journal of Farm Economics* 19: 603.

————— . 1937c. "Settlement and Unsettlement in the Resettlement Administration Program." *Law and Contemporary Problems* 4: 456-472.

————— . 1937-38. Review of Simon: *The Share-Cropper*. *Southwestern Social Science Quarterly* 18: 276-279.

————— . 1938-39. Review of *Works Progress Administration: Farmers on Relief and Rehabilitation*. *Southwestern Social Science Quarterly* 19: 106-108.

————— . 1939a. "The Rust Mechanical Cotton Picker and Probable Land-Use Adjustments." *Journal of Land and Public Utility Economics* 15: 155-166.

————— . 1939b. "The Cultivated Mind and the Cultivated Land in the Preservation of Democracy." Annual meetings of the Southwestern Social Science Association.

————— . 1940-41. "Review of Baker and McNeely: *Land Tenure in Arkansas, 1. The Farm Tenancy Situation. Southwestern Social Science Quarterly* 21: 285.

————— . 1941. "Is it Socially Desirable that Agricultural Production be Carried on Efficiently? If so, What Should Happen to the People Not Needed in Agricultural Production?" Annual Meeting, Texas Social Welfare Association.

————— . 1944. "Agriculture As an Economic Resource" and "Report of the Discussion Groups on Rural Communities and Towns Up To 2,500 Population." Pp. 29-33 and 59-61 in *The City-The Town-and the Community of Texas*. Proceedings of the University of Texas Conference on the Problems of The City-The Town-and the Community of Texas, Austin, October 5-6, 1944. Austin: University of Texas.

————. 1946a. "Lower Tax Rates for Capacity Output." Pp. 103-104 in *Planning for Jobs*, edited by Lyle Fitch and Horace Taylor. Philadelphia: Blakiston.

————. 1946b. "Technological Determinants of the Agricultural 'Way of Life'." *Proceedings*. Annual Meeting of the Texas Agricultural Workers' Association, pg. 91-96.

————. 1948. "The Essential Principles Which Should be Observed by Economists as Counselors on the Development of Legislation Governing Agriculture." Annual meetings of the Southwestern Social Science Association.

————. 1948a. "A Conversion Program for Southern Agriculture." Seminar, Department of Economics, University of Texas.

————. 1949. "Cotton in an Agricultural Program." *Proceedings*. Tenth Cotton Research Congress, Statewide Cotton Committee of Texas pp. 47-54.

————. 1950. "Agricultural Surpluses—Historical and Institutional Approach."Annual meetings of the Southwestern Social Science Association.

————. 1953-54. Comment on "Water Development as an Important Factor in the Utilization of the High Plains of Texas." *Southwestern Social Science Quarterly* 34: 60-64.

Wiley, G. A. 1992. Letter to Vaughn, September 3.

Wiley, J. M., 1992-93. Telephone interviews, August 21 and 22, 1992, and January 26, 1993.

Williams, E. 1944. *Application of the Instrumental Theory of Value to Agricultural Economics*, M.A. thesis. Austin: University of Texas.

Wolfe, A. B. 1916. *Readings in Social Problems*. Boston: Ginn.

Wolfe, A. B. 1920. "The Teaching of Economics Again." *Journal of Political Economy* 28: 735-753.

————. 1923. *Conservatism, Radicalism, and Scientific Method: An Essay on Social Attitudes*. New York: MacMillan.

Wooten, H. H., and Anderson, J. R. 1957. *Major Uses of Land in the United States: Summary for 1954*, Agricultural Information Bulletin No. 168, Agricultural Research Service. Washington DC: U.S. Department of Agriculture.

Zimmermann, E. W. 1911. *Die Britische Kohlenausfuhr, ihre Geschichte, Organisation and Bedeutung*. Essen, Ruhr: Druck von W. Girardet.

————. 1917. *Foreign Trade and Shipping*. New York: Alexander Hamilton Institute.

————. 1917. *Merchant Marine and Coal Export*. Modern Business Report. New York: Alexander Hamilton Institute.

————. 1918. *Recent Developments in Our Trade with South America*. Modern Business Report. New York: Alexander Hamilton Institute.

————. 1920-1921. "Why America's Export Coal Business Should Be Built Up." *Coal Age*, December 1920 (Part I) and January 1921 (Part II).

————. 1921. *Zimmermann on Ocean Shipping*. New York: Prentice-Hall, Inc.

————. 1922. "Shall We Subsidize our Ships? *Commerce and Finance*, XI, 23 (June 7).

————. 1924. "Economic Resources of the South Atlantic Area." *Proceedings of the National Foreign Trade Convention*. New York: National Foreign Trade Council.

————. 1926. "The Northwestern Fuel Problem, with Special Reference to the States of North and South Dakota and Adjoining Territory." *Investigations of the Preparation and Use of Lignite*. Washington: U. S. Bureau of Mines.

————. 1927a. "The Farm Surplus Problem: the Economic Paradox." *Barron's*, VII 17 (April 25).

————. 1927b. "Understanding the Farm Surplus Problem." *Barron's*, 23 (June 6).

————. 1927c. "The Crisis in the Petroleum Industry." *Editorial Research Reports* (June 6).

————. 1927d. "Oil Conservation and Stabilization." *Editorial Research Reports* (June 8).

————. 1927e. "The Agricultural Problem of the United States." *Editorial Research Reports* (December 17).

————. 1927f. "Background of the Agricultural Problem." *Editorial Research Reports* (December 24).

————. Victor S. Clark and associates 1930. *Puerto Rico and Its Problems*. Washington: The Brookings Institution. Zimmermann main contributor to chapter on "Commercial Organization;" also a contributor to chapter on "External Trade and Financial Relations."

————. 1931a. "International Economic Relations: Discussion." *The American Economic Review* 21(1): Supplement (March).

————. 1931b. "The Resource Hierachy of Modern World Economy." *Weltwirtschaftliches Archiv* 33 (April).

————. 1933a. *World Resources and Industries: a Functional Appraisal of the Availability of Agricultural and Industrial Resources*. New York: Harper and Brothers.

————. 1933b. "Natural Resources." *Encyclopedia of the Social Sciences* 11 (1933). "Resources of the South." *The South Atlantic Quarterly*, (July).

_____ . 1934. "The Relationship between Output of Work and Economic Well-being." *The American Economic Review* 24, 2(June).

_____ . 1935. "Wood Industries." *Encyclopedia of the Social Sciences*, 15.

_____ . 1936. "Resources." Chapter 7, Vol. 1, *Economic Principles and Problems* (3rd Ed.), edited by W. E. Spahr. New York: Farrar and Rinehart.

_____ . 1938. "The Relationship Between Population Density and the Manner of Land Utilization (or Exploitation) in Colonial Regions." *International Congress of Geography*.

_____ . 1940. *Staff Report to the International Committee on Puerto Rico.* Washington: U. S. Interdepartmental Committee on Puerto Rico, September 9, 1940.

_____ . 1944a. "What We Mean by Resources." *Texas Looks Ahead*, Vol. 1 of *The Resources of Texas*, edited by Lorene Drummond. Austin: The University of Texas.

_____ . 1944b. "All of Them Together." *Texas Looks Ahead*, Vol. 1 of *The Resources of Texas*, edited by Lorene Drummond. Austin: The University of Texas.

_____ . 1944c. "Resources—an Evolving Concept." *Proceedings and Transactions of the Texas Academy of Science*, 28.

_____ . 1946a. "Lo Que Debemos Entender por Recursos." *Investigacion Economica* 5(4).

_____ . 1946b. "Resources of Latin America, A Study in Methodology." *Some Economic Aspects of Postwar Inter-American Relations*. Austin: The University of Texas Institute of Latin American Studies.

_____ . 1951. *World Resources and Industries: A Functional Appraisal of the Availability of Agricultural and Industrial Materials*, (Rev. Ed). New York: Harper and Row.

_____ . 1957a. *Conservation in the Production of Petroleum: A Study in Industrial Control*. Petroleum Monograph Series, Vol. 2. New Haven: Yale University Press.

_____ . 1957b. *Recursos e Industrias del Mundo*. Mexico: Fondo de Cultura Economica.

_____ . 1964. *Introduction to World Resources*. Reprint of first ten chapters of *World Resources and Industries*, edited by Henry L. Hunker. New York: Harper and Row.

SUBJECT/AUTHOR INDEX

Agri-business, 163
Agricultural economics: Wiley's
     courses, 111-114, 116-118;
     Williams's thesis 124; Wis-
     consin 128; Committee on
     the Southwest economy
     145
Agriculture: cooperatives 56; inte-
     grating into the aggregate
     economy 116-119, 148; Fos-
     ter on public policy 123-
     125, McDonald's disserta-
     tion 127; Wiley's disserta-
     tion 129-131, Montgomery
     on 133; industrial society
     141; saving the economy
     144; Zimmermann 161;
     162-164
Allen, Ruth A. 1, 2, 4, 58, biogra-
     phical sketch 75, 76; 77-
     106, 180
Allen v. Darcy, 58
American Farm Economic Associa-
     tion, 114
American Petroleum Institute, 174
Amherst College 9
Ancient and Honorable Order of
     Flint Workers, 60
Armstrong, Bettie M., 131
Arnold, Thurman, 2

Ayres, Clarence E.: 1, 2, 4, biogra-
     phical sketch 7-11; Dewey
     13; dualisms 16-18; eco-
     nomic progress 21-27, 73,
     77; 107, Wiley 120, 121-124;
     126, 127, 133, Committee
     on the Southwest Economy
     145-147; 160, Zimmermann
     180, 181

Bankers, 36
Banking system, 36, 37, 41
Barriers to exit, 56
Beckwith, Burnham C., 66
Benedict, Harry Y., 110, 116
Berle, Adolf, 2
Brain Trust, 3, 14
Breit, William, 3, 28, 48, 72, 73
Business enterprise, 12, 63, 141

Capacity commitments, 56
Capital formation, 21, 173, 179
Clark, John Maurice, 8
Clark, John Bates 8, 34, 109
Class, 38, 81, 83, 88, 156, 161, 165
Classical economists, 34, 114
Cleveland, Grover, 97
Commission on Graduate Educa-
     tion in Economics, 31
Commons, John R., 2, Hale 33, 39,
     49; on real values 35; tradi-
     tion 48; Allen 76

197

competition: price 13; perfect 18;
    scarcity 46; agriculture 53,
    industrial organization 54-
    55; failures 57; free 59, 62;
    utility market 68; Montgo-
    mery 72; farmers 91, 92;
    sports 108; government
    113; societal arts 159
Concentration-and-control strategy,
    13
Conservation: programs 117; soil
    137; project 139; United
    Nations 156; nonrenewa-
    bility 161; petroleum 164,
    167-170; Zimmermann 172-
    176, 179, 180, 182
Cooperative movement, 54
Cooperatives, 55, 71, 130, 133
Corporate capitalism, 12
Cotton: cooperatives 54-57, 59, 61-
    63, 71, 133; women 75, 77-
    79; 88-94, 102, 103, 104,
    108; Wiley 120, 121; grow-
    ers 134; prices 136; Belt 137;
    141-145
Cotton market, 54-56, 62
Cowboy strike, 95, 101
Credit, 36, 37, 41, rural 109; farm
    114, 118, 119, 129 130, 162,
    163
Culture, 15, 17-19, 27, 28, economic
    51; 77, 117, 121, 127, 142,
    143, 158

Democracy, 16, 63, 71, 115, 143
Development: technological 4; 11,
    12, science 15; economic
    38, 46, 47, 122, 123, 128,
    133, 145, 152; stage 113; oil
    deposits 177-179
Dewey, John, 4, 8, 10, 14-16, 160
Dichotomy, 4, 10-12, 14, 127
Douglas, Paul H. 75

Dualism, 127
Duval, Claiborne Alexander, 134,
    135, 141

Earth-Man, 71
Eastern financial establishment, 58
Economancy, 170
Economic growth, 46, 47, 180
Economic process, 12, 13
Economic progress, 10, 23, 24, 26,
    121
Economic value of children, 83
Economization, 169, 170
Efficiency, 65, 92, allocative 119,
    123; 125, technological 127;
    135, 141, 144, 149, 174-176
Emulation, 14
Energy, 61, 63, 158, 160-164, 168,
    173
Erickson, Maurice, 52, 53, 72-74
Ethnocentrism, 17
Evans, Bert M., 113, 124-126, 141,
    147
Extra-routine housework, 84
Ezekial, Mordecai 2

Fair value, 68
Family farm, 86, 162-164
Farm cooperatives, 130
Farmers: Great Depression 13, 14;
    purchasing power 24; pro-
    duction methods 55; cotton
    93; organizations 118, 119;
    technology 129, 130, 131;
    loans 136, 137, Agricultural
    Adjustment Administra-
    tion 141-145; output 162,
    163; prices 176
Federal Oil Conservation Board,
    182
Field, James Alfred, 111
Foster, J. Fagg, 122-124
Free trade, 38, 40, 45, 46

Fuller, Joseph V., 97, 115, 138, 149
Fusion, 126-128

German historical school, 77
Gilman, Charlotte Perkins, 105
Gold standard, 35, 36
Gould, Jay, 96
Great Depression, 1, 14, 26, 38, 58, 60, 72, 167, 176
Growth theory, 20
Guaranteed annual income, 26

Habit, 20, 22, 23, 53, 78, 102, 105, 110
Hale, Edward Everett, 1, 4, biographical sketch 32; 33-49, 146, 147, 180
Hamilton, Walton, 2, 8, 13
Hotelling, Harold, 66, 176
Hegemony, 25
Heterodox economics, 8
Hibbard, Benjamin H., 114, 128
Home production, 85-87, 94, 102, 103
Hope Natural Gas Co., 68
Hoxie, Robert, 8
Human capital, 2, 21, 43, 170, 173

Industrial Revolution, 38, 160, 161, 164
Innovation, 70, 159, 168
Institutional adjustment, 21-23, 27, 46
Institutional economics: Tugwell 13; 20, premature death 28; 54, Wisconsin 112, 115; 131
Institutions: 3, economic 22, 71, 72; resistance 27; 31, market 53; technology 60, 63, 64; 77, rural 109; agricultural credit 118, 119, 121; Zimmermann 152; social 158, 159, 160, 162; 179, 181

Instrumentalism, 123
Integrated economy: Wiley and Wisconsin 112, 113, 115, 119; McDonald's dissertation 126, 127; 131, 135, 140, 142, 148, 149
Intellectual nihilism, 16
Invention, 35, 170
Invidious interest, 14
Irons, Martin, 96-98, 101
Irrationality, 93
Ise, John, 53

Jefferson, Thomas, 58, 63, 64
Jevons, Stanley, 37, 39, 40, 44, 45, 48, 49
Johnson, Alvin, 8
Johnson, D. Gale, 181
Johnson, Emory J., 67

Kahn, Alfred, 66
Keynes, John Maynard, 24, 33, 37, 38, 41-43, 49
Keyserling, Leon, 145
Kiekhofer, William H., 114, 128
Kirkendall, Richard S., 115, 119
Knight, Frank, 4, 75
Knights of Labor, 96

Labor theory of value, 19
Laissez faire, 3, 63, 164, 165, 173
Lingelbach, William Ezra 111
Long-run average cost, 69
Lubin, Isadore, 2
Lumber workers, 77, 78, 98, 99, 101, 102, 106

Macklin, Theodore, 115, 128
Managed currency, 36, 37
Managed trade, 45, 46
Marginal cost pricing, 2, 65-68, 70
Marginalist school, 38, 40
Market: capitalist 11, 12, 17-19;

institutions 53-57, 59, 62;
labor 77, 100-102; home
production 86, 88, 89, 93,
94; 121, price 134, 145; 166,
169, 171, 178, 180, demand
174; 175
Marshall, Alfred, 34, 37, 39, 40, 67
Marx, Karl, 19, 33, 37-39, 41, 42, 47-
49
Marxism, 146
Mathematics 40, 45, 52
Maverick, Samuel, 1, 2
McDonald, Stephen L., 107, 114,
dissertation 126, 127, 134;
147
Means, Gardiner, 2, 59
Meikeljohn, Alexander, 9
Mercantilism, 38
Metaphysical preconceptions, 34
Microeconomic theory, 46, 69
Miller, Edmund T., 32, 115, 116
Millis, Harry Alvin, 75, 111
Mints, Lloyd W., 75
Missouri Pacific Railroad, 96
Mitchell, Wesley C., 2, 8
Money-values, 35
Monopoly: unregulated 53, 54, 57-
60, 63, 64; 71, 72, 74, power
96, 98; 113
Monopoly capital, 98
Montgomery, Robert H.: biogra-
phical sketch 51-54; 55-74,
promotion to full professor
115; Wiley 132-134, 136,
137, 142, 146, 147
Moral agnosticism, 16
Munkirs, John, 61
Myth, 73, 95, 129

National Bureau of Economic
Research, 155
Nationalization of banking, 43
Neoclassical price theory, 122

New Deal, 2, 3, 14, 23, 24, 44, 130,
133, 135, 139, 142, 146, 176
New institutional economics, 3, 46,
47
Non-invidious interest, 14
North, Douglass, 3, 46, 47

OPEC, 178, 182
Overproduction, 79, 93

Peach, Nelson, 157
petroleum: conservation 156;
resource 158, 159; indus-
trial revolution 161; 164,
optimal degree of conservation 172-174, 176
Physiocrats, 34
Pigou, Alfred, 67
Power: 11-14, market 17; 19, 20,
social system 22-24; pur-
chasing 26; countervailing
28; purchasing 36, 117, 142;
38, 46, 47, corruptive 64;
monopoly 96, 113; 158
Preferences, 12, 16, 18-20
Prices: oligopoly 13; 14, market 18;
relative 18, 19, 21; global
36; nonuniform 54-57; 59,
63, 66, cotton 89, 136; 117,
127, 129, 130, 145, real 162;
mineral 165-167; 173, stabilize 176-179
Public ownership, 65, 67
Public utilities, 133, 134
Puerto Rico, 154, 155

Railroads, 61, 65, 67, 70, 96, 134
Reciprocity, 128, 129
Regulation: 12, bank 43; utility 54,
57, 64, 67, 71, theory of 61,
price 66, petroleum 167,
168, 174-177, 179
Reid, Margaret, 105

Relative prices, 18, 19, 165
Reserves: petroleum 165, 166, 171, 173, 178
Resettlement Administration, 124, 135-140
Resources: 2, 5, corporate concentration 13, 14; 19-22, scarce 25, 63, 66, 115, world 123, 124, 125; agricultural 129, 140, 143, entrepreneurial 148, natural 152, 154-161, 164-173; conserve 175-180, 182, 183
Resourceship, 151, 152, 157, 158, 160, 161, 164, 172, 173, 179, 180, 182
Ricardo, David, 38-41
Richardson, Jean, 125, 132, 149
Roosevelt, Franklin, 3, 35-37, 117, 135, 147, 148, 155
Roosevelt administration, 35, 117
Rules of the game, 46

Saunders, Allan F., 115
Scherer, Frederick, 70, 74
Scott, William A., 114, 128
Shine, Mary L., 114
Smelser, Neil J., 127, 128
Smyth v. Ames, 68
Social process, 18, 19, 22
Social values, 35
Socialism, 41
Socialization of lending, 43
Status: social 11, 12, 14, 21-23, women 76, 87; economic 80, 81, 83, 94; marital 88, 96
Status quo, 19, 53, 159
Stocking, George W., 2, 115
Sulfur market, 57
Sunk costs, 56

Tastes, 18, 19

Taussig, Frank, 67
Taylor, Henry C. 108, 111, 136
Technological change, 3, 20, 27, 48, 118, 159
Technology and society: 4, 11, 12, wants and 20; 22, "old" institutionalism 47; 58, 60, cost-saving 65, 69-71; 121-125, industrial 129; 133, 152, new 159; 160, 161, 162, 165, 168
Texas: University of, 9, 32, 49, 133-138, 145-147, 155-157; 57, poker 58; 80, cotton 90, 93, organized labor 95, 96, 98-102; Board of Regents 115, 140
Texas school, 25, 48, 51-54, 73, 74, 105, 152, 180, 181
Trade, 14, 36, 38, 40, 43, 45, 46, 128, 129, 153, 154
Tugwell, Rexford G., 13, 14, 24
Tyson, Laura D'Andrea, 43, 46

United Mine Workers, 95
United States: 49, automobiles 70; history of labor 76; monopoly capital 98, 99; rural life 109, 110; economic integration 126, 128; cash crop 141; Zimmermann 153, 155
Unitization, 175
Unpaid labor, 79, 80, 88-90, 93

Veblen, Thorstein: 2, 4, 8, legacy 10-14; 17, Tugwell 24, 25; Montgomery 53; Allen 77; 87, Wiley 110; 127, 160
Veblenian dichotomy, 10, 11
Veblenian waste, 14, 25
Vested interests, 19, 23
Vickrey, William, 66
Viner, Jacob, 69
von Thunen, Johann Heinrich, 114

Wallace, Henry, 2, 148
Wants, 18-22, 151, 157, 158
War, 33, 49, 57, 96, 98, 112, 153
Waste, 14, 25, 165-168, 173, 175
Wehrwein, George S., 114, 133, 138
Wells, Oris V., 130
Wiley, Clarence Alton, 1, 4, 5, 107-
    138, 140-149, 162, 180, 181
Williams, Elgin, 124

Wolfe, Albert Benedict, 110, 111
World War I, 33, 52, 108, 128, 132
World War II, 52, 65, 72, 82, 117,
    121, 124, 127, 139, 143, 155,
    163

Zimmermann, Erich W., 1, 2, 5,
    123, 151-165, 167-183